SHEPHERD OF JERUSALEM

SHEPHERD OF JERUSALEM

A BIOGRAPHY OF

Rabbi Abraham Isaac Kook

By

DOV PERETZ ELKINS

JASON ARONSON INC.

Northvale, New Jersey

London

First Jason Aronson Inc. Softcover Edition—1995

10 9 8 7 6 5 4 3 2 1

Library of Congress Cataloging-in-Publication Data

Elkins, Dov Peretz.
Shepherd of Jerusalem : a biography of Rabbi Abraham Isaac Kook / by Dov Peretz Elkins. — 1st Jason Aronson Inc. ed.
p. cm.
Previously published: New York : Shengold, 1975.
Summary: A biography of the rabbi active in the Zionist movement that founded the independent Jewish state of Israel.
ISBN 1-56821-597-5 (alk. paper)
1. Kook, Abraham Isaac, 1865–1935—Juvenile literature. 2. Rabbis—Biography—Juvenile literature. 3. Religious Zionists—Biography—Juvenile literature. [1. Kook, Abraham Isaac, 1865–1935. 2. Rabbis. 3. Zionists.] I. Title.
BM755.K66E44 1995
296.6'1—dc20
[B] 95-8311
CIP
AC

Manufactured in the United States of America. Jason Aronson Inc. offers books and cassettes. For information and catalog write to Jason Aronson Inc., 230 Livingston Street, Northvale, New Jersey 07647.

For Lee Dushoff
Friend and confidant for a quarter century
For Harvey Cedars, and others times and other places
and for Elaine Dushoff
for that and more . . . .

ACKNOWLEDGMENTS

Deepest appreciation is extended to Frank Brezel, Dr. Azriel Eisenberg, and Deborah Karp who read the manuscript and offered advice and encouragement; to Sylvia Landress of the Zionist Library and Archives for supplying much bibliographic material; to Rabbi Jacob Agus for permission to quote passages from his book, *Banner of Jerusalem;* to Pearl Ostroff for her boundless devotion and infinite patience; to Hillel and Jonathan Elkins for reading the proofs; to Justin Vigdor for his encouragement and friendship; and especially to Moshe Sheinbaum of Shengold Publishers who worked with me very closely in every step of the publication of this volume.

We gratefully acknowledge the Zionist Archives and Library for providing us with the photographs of Rabbi A. I. Kook.

CONTENTS

CONTENTS

1

THE BOY WHO WANTED TO BE A KOHEN

Nine-year-old Abraham always sat alone in a corner of the classroom, poring over the huge pages of the Talmud, humming the ancient Hebrew and Aramaic words that filled its pages.

The other children studied in pairs, each consisting of one younger child and an older student acting as his teacher. This is how the Jewish children in Russia studied at the *cheder*. The students sat in a small, poorly lit room from the early hours of the morning until late into the night, pausing only when someone reminded them it was time to eat.

But Abraham sat alone. Was he being shunned by his fellow students because of something he did? Not at all. On the contrary, he was being honored. His teachers had decided that he was so far ahead of the others that studying with them would hold him back. And so he sat alone, studying the writings of pious Jews of centuries ago, mastering tractate after tractate of the Talmud.

No one forced young Abraham to spend so many of his waking hours increasing his knowledge and sharpening his mind.He did it on his own, because he wanted to. This was the only life he knew. His father, his grandfather, and his great-grandfather had all been scholars in the law and lore of Judaism.

Abraham lived in the town of Grieva, a province in northwestern Russia. All the people in the town of Grieva were Jewish, except for the police and government officials. Many of the people were merchants, businessmen, and artisans; others were rabbis, scholars, and students of the Law: the Bible, the Codes, and the Talmud. All of them, however, regardless of occupation, were devoted to the study of the Torah and other sacred writings of Judaism. Even when they worked, they would spend their lunch hour poring over the folios of the Talmud, and chanting it aloud to help them memorize it. Though all of them were religious and learned, they were not as learned as the rabbis and students who studied all of the time.

All of the Jews in Grieva dressed alike. Their coats were of black gabardine and their hats, or *shtreimels*, were made of fur. Their chins were hidden behind thick beards. The women covered their heads with *sheitels*, wigs, a sign of modesty, because married women were not supposed to appear in public with their hair uncovered.

None of the Jewish townsmen were wealthy. All they wanted from life was to know the will of God and to try their best to fulfill it. To do this they spent every spare moment studying the sacred Scriptures, and they chanted the traditional prayers three times daily. Although their physical possessions were few, they were able to live happy lives because they could do what pleased them most: study and pray.

Abraham's father was Rabbi Shlomo Zalman Kook; his mother, Pearl, was the daughter of Rabbi Raphael, who was both a businessman and a scholar. His middle name, Isaac, was the name of another great-grandfather, Rabbi Isaac, one of the first followers of the great and famous sage, Rabbi

Israel Baal Shem Tov, founder of the movement of *Hasidism*.

The *Hasidim*, or pious ones, believed in emotional expression of their religious faith, through joyful singing and dancing. It was not enough for them to study and pray; religion for them had to be filled with great happiness and merriment, expressing thanks to God for all the world's blessings.

After the beginning of Hasidism, an opposing movement sprung forth, whose members were called *Mitnagdim*, or "opponents." They felt that study was to have the main emphasis in Jewish life and that too much singing and dancing led to light-heartedness and lack of zeal for study.

Young Abraham had ancestors from both of these groups, the *Hasidim* and the *Mitnagdim*, and he enjoyed both life-styles. He loved to study, and also to openly express his joy over life and its blessings.

Abraham Isaac Kook was born in the summer of 1865. When he was 8 days old, his family celebrated his *Brit Milah*, a ceremony in which a male is initiated into the family of the Jewish people. It is both a symbol and a covenant of faithfulness between God and the Jewish people, and was first introduced to the patriarch Abraham as related in the biblical book of Genesis.

After the ceremony, when all the friends and relatives were merrily drinking wine and eating cake, Abraham's mother held up a tiny baby's garment and called for everyone's attention.

"I am now going to sew a very important button on little Abraham's gown," she explained. Everyone gazed with rapt attention at the button.

"This button," she continued, "was given to me by my grandfather, who received it from his father, a very pious and humble student of the Torah. It will adorn Abraham's garment, so that he might receive some of the saintliness of his ancestor.

"I am also making him a *yarmulka* (skull cap) from the cloth of his ancestor's coat. May our son Abraham be as devoted to the priceless and ancient heritage of Judaism as his pious grandfather."

As Abraham grew older, this *yarmulka* was one of the things he treasured most. His mother could not get him to go to sleep without it.

Abraham began to learn Hebrew from the moment he was able to talk. The first words he uttered were those of the Torah, "Moses commanded us with the rules of the Torah, which is the heritage of the congregation of Jacob."

By the time he was four, Abraham was studying the Bible. He began with the Book of Leviticus, the third book of the Torah. This is customary among the Jewish people because Leviticus deals with laws of purity, and it is only fitting that they be studied by the pure souls of young children.

But for the Kook family, the Book of Leviticus had much greater meaning, because it also describes the various animal sacrifices which the *Kohanim* (Priests) were responsible for in the desert during the journey to the promised land, and in the ancient Temple in Jerusalem. The Kook family were members of the *Kohanim*. The *Kohanim* were descendants of Aaron, the brother of Moses, who was appointed by God as the first High Priest of the Jewish people. This priesthood was designated solely to Aaron and his descendants and only they were allowed to accept the people's sacrifices and offer them at the holy altar. It was also their duty to know all the laws concerning the sacrifices as described in the Book of Leviticus. The last of these sacrifices were offered in the Temple in Jerusalem, which was destroyed by the Roman conquerors in the year 70 C.E. Only a small section of the Temple's surrounding wall remains standing to this day. It is known as " the Wailing Wall" and "Western Wall," and is located in the old section of Jerusalem.

Abraham's father often shared with his son his hope for the immediate restoration of the Temple. "We must always be ready," he would say, "to perform all the duties of the Temple, for we will never know when God may choose to rebuild it."

Nevertheless, the spirit of the glorious days of the Temple was always rekindled in Grieva on the Sabbath, when all work stopped. Everyone wore his best garments and spent most of the day in the synagogue, praying. Between prayers, the townsmen would study, father with son.

Once, when Abraham's young friends had finished studying, they came to visit him. As they entered his home, they overheard a conversation in a language that sounded strange to them, yet somewhat familiar. They knew it was not Russian or Yiddish, which were the languages they spoke. "What are they speaking" they asked one another. Suddenly, one of the boys recognized the language. "Why it's Hebrew," he said, "the holy language! The language of the Torah!"

Although all Jewish children throughout Russia and Poland studied Hebrew, it was not common to hear it spoken. Hebrew was reserved mainly for the study of the Bible, and for praying. But Abraham's father wanted the sacred language to be part of his son's very being, and reading it was therefore not sufficient. So on a holy day, like the Sabbath, Abraham and his father would speak in Hebrew to each other. Abraham's love for Hebrew never ceased. It soon became his second mother-tounge, and his ability to speak it fluently became extrmely useful to later in his life.

At the age of seven, Abraham Isaac Kook took up a very difficult task: the study of the Talmud. The Talmud is a collection of writings of sages and rabbis written during six centuries and edited around 540 C.E. It is divided into six sections and more than sixty sub-sections. Its words fill thousands of pages and it is always studied together with commentaries, which explain its meaning and content. Since there is so much meaning behind each phrase and word in the Talmud, studying it is slow, difficult and painstaking.

After Abraham had completed two years of studying the Talmud, his father was extremely proud of his progress. Not only was he mastering the meaning of the Talmud, but he was also mastering the Hebrew and Aramaic languages in which the Talmud was written. "You have learned a great deal," Abraham's father said to him. "The people of Grieva are beginning to call you an *Illui* (genius)."

Abraham's memory was so retentive that he rarely had to read a passage more than once to remember it. His superior intelligence, combined with his constant devotion to study, and his zealous concentration on the most minute details of the Law, enabled him to achieve phenomenal success in his studies.

For this reason, by the time he was only nine years old, Abraham was given his own desk in the *Bet Hamidrash*, the synagogue's study hall, where all of the students sat and studied the Talmud in pairs. Whenever Abraham entered the room, the other students would turn towards him and whisper to one another: "There is the *Illui*, the genius, Abraham Isaac, the son of Shlomo Kalman, the *Kohen*."

Through all of his studies, Abraham kept in mind the fact that he was a *Kohen*, for this ancestry imposed upon him the special obligation of knowing all the laws of the Temple should it be restored in his lifetime. Abraham prayed each day of his life for the privilege of serving as a *Kohen* in the restored Temple.

2

PRAYING FOR THE REDEMPTION

Through the words of the prayerbook, Jews all over the world expressed their longing to see the restoration of the Holy City, Jerusalem, and the redemption of the Jewish people. They uttered this wish three times daily.

To young Abraham, this redemption would provide him with the opportunity to serve as *Kohen* in the temple. He was very proud of this and studied all the books about the priesthood and the sacrifices with dedication and love. After all, not everyone could serve in the holy temple as God's special servant.

It was this faith in the coming of the redemption that kept alive the hope of all Jewry. For centuries the Jews had been persecuted and massacred in large numbers. Since the year 70 C.E., when they lost their national independence, they had had no permanent home. No country would accept them as full citizens and even when they did achieve a modicum of acceptance, it did not last long. Inevitably, the closest friends of the Jews soon became their enemies and drove them into exile, forcing them to roam from land to land in search of shelter.

In Russia and Eastern Europe there were many small, concentrated Jewish communities like Grieva. The Jews had to live together because the Gentile world was hostile to them. They could not find acceptance by anyone but their own people. And so they lived in isolated, withdrawn communities, always harboring the hope that God would soon redeem them and return them to their own home land, *Eretz Yisrael*, the Land of Israel, given by God to Abraham, Isaac, and Jacob.

The phrase "Eretz Yisrael" was a frequent household expression in these communities. Even though it was far away, and most had never seen it in person, it was very real to them. They felt that the redemption and the return to Eretz Yisrael could happen any day.

One day Abraham's parents saw him playing outside with other children. He was standing in front of them, lining them up in a straight line, and showing them how to raise their right hand and imagine that they were carrying a heavy bundle on their back. His parents wondered what it was all about.

Abraham's father stepped outside the house and moved close enough to the children to hear what they were saying. "March! March!" he heard Abraham shout, "off to Eretz Yisrael!"

His father laughed, but was not surprised, because it was natural to want to go to Eretz Yisrael. All of the adults did. Naturally, the children did, too.

"Where did he learn such a game, Pearl?" asked Rabbi Shlomo. "Already at such an early age he wants to migrate to Eretz Yisrael!"

"Of course he does, Shlomo. How could he help it, living in this house and in this town? And does he not mention the rebuilding of Jerusalem in the Birkat Hamazon (Grace after Meals) at least three times every day, and again during the daily prayers in the morning, noon, and evening? And don't you think he's aware of the charity box hanging on the wall for contributions to the people living in Eretz Yisrael?"

In Jewish homes it was customary each Friday, at the approach of the Sabbath, to empty the coat pockets and drop coins in a charity box designated for Eretz Yisrael. As families did so, they made a silent prayer that their time would come, too, to be among the fortunate ones living in the Holy Land.

Pearl continued to explain to her husband how natural it was for Abraham to love Eretz Yisrael. "Don't you remember when my father, may he rest in peace, passed away, and we placed some soil from the Holy Land in the coffin? Moments before, Abraham asked me why I was carrying a bag of dirt to the funeral, and I explained to him that since his grandfather could not be buried in Eretz Yisrael, the next best thing was to have some of the holy soil lie beneath him."

"You are right, Pearl," said Rabbi Shlomo, "how could he not love Eretz Yisrael?"

OFF TO LUTZIN

By age fifteen, Abraham's knowledge had grown in breadth and depth. He knew more books of the Talmud than anyone his age, and he understood them better. He had also learned a great deal about how to conduct the sacrificial services in the temple when the restoration would come. He was determined not to be caught unaware if he were to be called upon to officiate at the sacred altar.

In fact, he knew so much that his father felt it was time for him to seek out new teachers. "Go, my son," he bade the young lad, "to the town of Lutzin, where there are other teachers who can fill your thirst for knowledge. Here in Grieva, we can teach you no more than you already know."

Abraham gathered together the few garments he owned and tied them into a small bundle. He then threw them over his back and set out to nearby Lutzin to increase his knowledge of the Torah.

It was not easy to live in a strange town, with no family or friends. But the people there had heard of his fame as an *Illui* and made him feel at home. The teachers of Lutzin were thrilled to have a child prodigy grace their midst and be a model for their students and their own sons and daughters. His large bright eyes showed a warmth and sincerity that endeared him to his friends, neighbors and teachers.

Aided by the hospitality of the people of Lutzin, Abraham managed to progress in his studies. From the wee hours of the dawn, he would sit in the Academy and add more and more to the growing store-house of his knowledge.

Sometimes he would stay up all night to continue studying. On certain days of the week it was the custom of some pious Jews to exercise extra zeal by pursuing their studies through the night without any sleep. It was especially common to do this on holidays. Late into the night, everything was quiet, no voices or footsteps were heard in the street, and only the light of the candle on the desk illuminated the room, creating a very special mood that helped Abraham enjoy his studying even more.

One morning, some of the students entered the study hall and saw Abraham sitting in his customary place. On his arm and around his head were wrapped the *tefillin* (phylacteries), the black straps which bound to his body the little boxes containing parchments with sections of the Torah written on them. Covering his head and back was a large woolen *talis* (prayer shawl). His head was bent over the wooden table, and his eyes were closed in deep concentration.

"I think I see tears in his eyes," said one of the students. "I wonder what has happened to our friend Abraham."

"There's no need to worry," answered another. "Abraham is not shedding tears because he is sad, he is crying out of happiness. He is praying so fervently for the rebuilding of the holy Temple and for the opportunity to live in a restored Jerusalem and be surrounded by the holy air of Eretz

Yisrael, that the thought of this fulfillment brings tears of happiness to his eyes."

Young Abraham Isaac prayed, hoped, cried, and studied, all in the service of God and in anticipation of redemption. He was eventually to play a great role in that redemption. His family background, his ancestral history, his early community life in Eastern Europe, and his early intensive training in Torah knowledge and piety were to be the basic ingredients for making him a leader of his people in the future. One day, soon, his dreams were to come true. Meanwhile, Abraham had yet to come a few steps closer to realizing that dream.

3

A LITTLE CLOSER TO ZION

The same year Abraham arrived in Lutzin, a terrible series of events occured which were to change Jewish life in Russia, and strongly affect Abraham's life as well.

The new Russian Czar decided that he would no longer tolerate minority groups who did not totally assimilate to become exactly like all other Russians. He was dissatisfied with groups like the Jews, who preserved their ancestral customs and beliefs. They were not "Russian" enough for him.

All over Russia, Jewish communities felt the wrath of the Czar spreading over them like a plague. Random beatings, robbery, and murder were not uncommon.

These attacks and wholesale slaughters of Jews were known as *pogroms*. Jews experiencing the pogroms began to fear for their lives, and their once quiet and placid existence was beginning to crumble. They knew that it would not be too long before they would all be killed.

Groups of Jews throughout Russia and eastern Europe began to talk of deserting their homeland, which had become the center of many centuries of rich Jewish life, for a place free of persecution.

Naturally, their thoughts turned toward Mount Zion, the holy mount in Jerusalem where the glories of their ancient history were enacted. The word "Zion" became a symbol for the whole of Eretz Yisrael, just as Washington, D.C., is sometimes used to symbolize the United States, or London for all of England. Thus, the movement to re-establish a Jewish community in Zion took the name "Zionism."

Instead of merely *praying* for a return to Jerusalem, many Jews began to make actual plans for their own redemption. Some moved to Eretz Yisrael immediately and settled there. Small farm colonies were established, and Jews once again began, though in small numbers, to work the soil of their ancestors.

Abraham's uncle, Rabbi Mordecai Gimple Yaffe, was one of those who tired of living in the *Diaspora* (a general term for lands where Jews were dispersed, outside the Holy Land). He yearned deeply to live in a restored Eretz Yisrael and helped found a group known as *Hibat Zion,* Love of Zion.

Abraham was at home one Sabbath afternoon during a brief visit with his family, when Uncle Mordecai walked in the door.

"I have made a momentous decision," said Rabbi Yaffe to Abraham's father and mother. "I am going to move to Eretz Yisrael. I have heard that Baron Edmond de Rothschild of Paris has agreed to support a group of Jewish agricultural colonies and to construct wine cellars in them so the Jews would have an independent source of income. I have decided to join them, although I haven't yet decided which colony."

"Are you mad?" declared Rabbi Shlomo. "Don't you know that malaria is widespread there because the swamps have not been drained, and that the Arab bandits are constantly raiding Jewish settlements? It is too dangerous to return now. Wait until conditions are more peaceful and secure."

"There are several thousand of us, Shlomo," replied Rabbi Mordecai. "We cannot be stopped. We are familiar with all of the difficulties that will greet us, but, nevertheless, we can no longer bear to live at the mercy of the Czar. In Eretz Yisrael we will at least be able to fight for our rights, and protect ourselves. Even at this moment, Jewish fighting bands are being organized to protect the colonies."

Like Rabbi Mordecai, thousands of Jews made the difficult decision to migrate to what was then Palestine, in the early 1880's. They hoped to find a new way of life and an opportunity to create Jewish communities that would be independent, free and self-sustaining. The members of the group *Hibat Zion* were known as *Hovevai Zion* (Lovers of Zion).

When young Abraham heard his uncle's words, his eyes glistened with excitement. Maybe the *Hovevai Zion* were the ones who would touch off the beginning of the Redemption.

Some months later, letters arrived from a colony called *Yahud*, near Petach Tikvah. Among them was a letter from Uncle Mordecai which described the life in Eretz Yisrael as it really was in the late nineteenth century.

"I cannot say that it is easy here," he wrote. "We all face very serious dangers, even of death. We are living in the midst of an unfriendly Arab population, but at least we are beginning to defend ourselves. Our sense of pride in working the soil of our ancestors has lifted our spirits and given us renewed hope for the future. Some day, perhaps, we will have our own independent nation here as all the others peoples of the world have theirs."

With each new letter, Abraham felt closer and closer to Eretz Yisrael. It would be some time, though, before the moment would arrive for Abraham himself to join those living in the Holy Land. His path to Eretz Yisrael would not be a direct one, and many detours would delay his ultimate arrival in the Promised Land.

ON TO SMARGON

Soon thereafter, word reached the ears of Abraham about a new movement founded among Russian Jewry, known as the *Mussar* (Ethics) Movement. Its founder was Rabbi Israel Salanter of Lithuania. Abraham's teacher in the academy told him about it:

"It is said that in the town of Smargon there is a large group of people who belong to a Mussar movement. They set aside an hour a day to pore over books of morality and ethics, endeavoring to strengthen their character and way of life. They are zealous in the performance of all laws which affect the relationship of man to his fellow,laws such as loving one's neighbor, helping other people, care in not hurting feelings, being scrupulously honest, and so on."

The teacher's words aroused Abraham's interest in the group. "This sounds like a group I should know more about," he responded, "where can I find them?"

"If you go to Smargon," his teacher said, "you will find out more about the people who belong to this movement. You can leave to go whenever you wish."

Thus, at age eighteen, Abraham Isaac Kook moved to another town, Smargon. It did not take him long to become affiliated with the pious and saintly rabbis of the town who were members of the Movement. He spent many hours with them in prayer, reflection, and studies.

When Rabbi Israel Salanter died, Abraham was deeply affected. He performed the special rites of mourning prescribed for a student when his teacher leaves the world, and recited, with his fellow students, the special memorial prayer for a teacher: *Kaddish DeRabanan,* the Scholar's Kaddish. He also wore sackcloth and ashes as a sign of grief.

With the death of Rabbi Israel, Abraham finally felt that he was ready to go on to the greatest center of Jewish piety and scholarship in all of Russia, a city renowned for producing highly learned rabbis: Volozhin.

"Do you suppose I would be accepted in the Academy at Volozhin?" Abraham asked one of the rabbis who taught at his Yeshiva.

"Will you be accepted?" laughed the rabbi. "Why I received a letter just yesterday from the *Rosh Yeshiva* (Dean of the Academy), Rabbi Naftali Zvi Yehuda Berlin, saying that he had already heard about you and is anxious for you to come and study in Volozhin."

Abraham was shocked when he heard this. "The famous Rabbi Berlin wrote a letter about me?" he asked, jumping with excitement, "I must hurry and go to Volozhin immediately!"

4

THE END OF VOLOZHIN

When he arrived at the Yeshiva in Volozhin, Abraham reported to the office of the *Rosh Yeshiva,* Rabbi Naftali Zvi Yehuda Berlin. He was as known as the "Neziv," a Hebrew word meaning "Pillar," taken from the first letter of his names.

"Come in, Abraham," said Rabbi Berlin. "Please take a seat. We are very happy to have you here at Volozhin. I am sure you know that our Yeshiva was founded by Rabbi Chaim, the leading disciple of the Vilna Gaon, Rabbi Elijah. Since 1802, we have been the seat of Jewish learning for all eastern Europe."

"I know this," replied Abraham. "That is why I am especially thrilled and honored to be here."

The Volozhin Yeshiva was unsurpassed for its depth of learning and for the greatness of its rabbis and teachers. Over five hundred young men converged there from all over Russia to drink from this famous well-spring of Torah knowledge.

At Volozhin, Abraham Isaac felt closer than ever to his life's goals. As an outstanding student there, he became closely associated with the *Rosh Yeshiva,* Rabbi Berlin. The dean had a very strong influence on Abraham's thinking and feeling.

One day a group of Russian government officials paid a visit to the Yeshiva.

"We want you to expand your course of studies in this school, Rabbi Berlin. We want you to teach the Russian language and literature beside Hebrew and Talmud."

"But we are a Jewish school," protested Rabbi Berlin. "There are many other institutions that can teach Russian subjects. If we take time away from our study of the Torah, we will not be able to train our students properly."

A battle was waged between these two forces for many years. Rabbi Berlin refused to give in. Finally, he permitted one hour a week for a course in the Russian language, but the Russian government was still not satisfied. They insisted on more and more Russian secular studies, such as Russian literature, history and art. When they saw how Rabbi Berlin persisted in teaching only sacred subjects, they decided to close the Yeshiva. The closing finally came in 1892, after Abraham had already left.

While he studied at Volozhin, young Abraham increased his devotion to the way of life he loved best: listening to lectures of great masters, covering more and more ground in the Talmud, and intensifying his feelings for the Jewish faith. The environment in the Academy was so God-fearing that Abraham felt closer to his Maker each day. During his prayers he experienced a feeling of unusual tranquillity and the intense emotion one feels when witnessing a great sight in nature or reading a moving story or poem.

He once told Rabbi Berlin, "I feel here as if I were living in Eretz Yisrael."

HEBREW AND ZION

Part of Abraham's love for God and the Jewish way of

life was expressed through his strong feeling for the sacred tongue, Hebrew, and for the Holy Land, Eretz Yisrael. One afternoon, when the students were standing outside the Yeshiva doors chatting together, Abraham suddenly broke into the conversation in Hebrew.

"Why do you speak in the holy tongue?" demanded one of his comrades. "Don't you know that Hebrew is reserved for holy purposes and not for daily speech? Do you want to turn a sacred vessel into an everyday instrument of conversation? How else can Hebrew retain its holiness unless we use it only during holy moments?"

"All of life is holy," answered Abraham. "Our ancestors in the Bible used Hebrew in their daily speech, and it helped them become more holy. Besides, the Jews living in Eretz Yisrael now are beginning to speak Hebrew again. If these people, who are not rabbis, and many of whom are not as religious as ourselves, can speak Hebrew – then certainly we, here in the greatest Yeshiva in eastern Europe, must also speak Hebrew."

"Our people are witnessing the beginning of their redemption now. Jews all over Russia and eastern Europe are longing for a return to a normal, national life of their own. They are beginning to cast off the shackles of exile, and are reviving the ways of life of ancient days. How can we refrain from being a part of this movement?"

The argument became more heated as the time passed. At one point, another student turned to him and said, "We need not redeem ourselves. God will redeem us in His own good time. He does not need Abraham Isaac Kook or any *Hovevai Zion* to force his hand."

Abraham told him about his uncle, Rabbi Mordecai Gimple Yaffe, and the many other rabbis who believed that God would cause the redemption to come only when the people were prepared for it, when they lived in the Holy Land, and when they would return the sacred language of Hebrew to daily use as in biblical times.

The argument continued for a while, but then Abraham turned away in disgust. He could not convince them that he was right.

Rabbi Berlin, however, was in favor of the *Hovevai Zion*. He looked upon the young people who began to migrate to Palestine with an eye of sympathy and understanding. Although many of them were not religious, he believed that they were fulfilling a great divine commandment by settling in the Holy Land. God would, in his own way, inspire them to return to the Torah way of life.

Abraham was deeply influenced by this sympathetic attitude. While others scorned those youth who neglected their prayers and the Sabbath and holy days in pursuit of other cultures, Rabbi Berlin understood the conditions which caused this break-away from Judaism and thus reacted with sympathy, rather than scorn.

One day, Rabbi Berlin was lecturing to his students about the days of the Babylonian Exile in the sixth century, B.C.E.

"When our ancestors were driven by the Babylonians from their sacred homeland, many of them began to enjoy life in the great city of Babylon, with its famous hanging gardens and luxurious way of life. They began to desert Judaism. Then, fifty years after the destruction of Jerusalem, the Persians conquered Babylonia and permitted the Jews to return. Many were able to go back and rebuild their national life. At first many of them were not religious, but later teachers such as Ezra arrived who taught the Torah and restored them to their religious ways."

The students were able to see the parallel to their own times.

Rabbi Berlin soon started his own Zionist organization for young religious students of his Yeshiva at Volozhin. He called it *Nes Ziona* (Banner of Zion).

Since the Russian government forbade the existence of such organizations, it had to be kept secret. As part of the secret initiation ceremonies, each member had to take the following oath:

"I swear that I will be faithful to the goal of our society and to endeavor during the whole of our lifetime to strive for the realization of the ideal of the upbuilding of Eretz Yisrael, and not to divulge the secrets of the society to anyone before he too joins by oath."

Nevertheless, the crafty spies of the Russian government were somehow able to get information about the organization. In 1889, the police provided government authorities with documented evidence of the group's existence, and the society was forcibly disbanded soon thereafter.

While taking an active part in *Nes Ziona,* Abraham became aware of the importance of organizations and community support for Zionism and Judaism. He was soon to have his chance to take the lead in these areas in a new community.

5

ABRAHAM BECOMES A RABBI

A romance between a young man and woman in Volozhin can not be compared in any way with one in America.

In Volozhin, there was no dating, no time for "falling in love" before getting married. In fact, the marriage was arranged more according to the tastes of the fathers of the bride and groom than by their own.

Abraham concluded his studies at Volozhin with his ordination as a Rabbi. Shortly after the ordination ceremony, the rabbi of a nearby town approached Abraham. His name was Rabbi Elijah David Rabinowitz-Tomim and he was from the town of Ponivesh.

"I have heard many fine things about you, young man," he said in a deep, serious tone of voice. "In fact, they say that you are the most promising student to graduate from the Yeshiva."

"They are certainly exaggerating," replied Abraham. "I am merely trying to serve God in the best way I know how – by study, prayer, and good deeds."

"Nevertheless, your teachers predict great things for

your future. I would be privileged to have you as my son-in-law."

Abraham knew of Rabbi Tomim and wanted very much to marry the daughter of a pious and scholarly rabbi, a woman who would understand him and his way of life. He knew that from the home of a great man like Rabbi Tomim must emerge a woman of valor.

After a period of thought, and consultation with friends and teachers, Abraham decided that this would be a proper match. He did not know the young lady, but he trusted the mature judgment of his elders more than his own inexperienced and youthful tastes.

After the wedding, Abraham's father-in-law persuaded him to settle in Ponivesh.

"In our community," Rabbi Tomim convinced him, "you will be able to study without distraction. It will be my honor to offer you what meager means I have to support you during the early stage of your marriage. In this way you can continue your studies and prepare yourself for a career in the rabbinate."

Rabbi Kook was very happy to hear this, because he wanted to continue studying and, at the same time, observe a rabbi who was active in the community.

In Ponivesh, Abraham received his first practical experience in community affairs. Often his father-in-law would call upon him to fulfill minor chores. As time passed, he became more and more active in the town, but always devoted the major portion of his time to Torah study. He lectured to young students, taught difficult passages in the Talmud to individuals who came to him, and served as a kind of assistant rabbi to his wife's father. These were excellent experiences for the young rabbi.

The opportunity to work with his father-in-law permitted the youthful Rabbi Kook to meet some of the rabbis in the surrounding towns. He also became more familiarized with the conditions of the people in the community. His life was no longer confined within the four walls of the *Bet Hamidrash.*

The more he saw of the outside world, the more shocked he was at the extent that Judaism was being neglected by the masses. People went to their jobs and places of business on the Sabbath! Young children did not continue their Jewish education past age thirteen! Synagogue attendance was extremely poor.

In conversations with his colleagues, he sensed a feeling of apathy towards these "heretics."

"How can you neglect the stray sheep from the Jewish fold?" he would admonish them.

"They do not deserve our attention," was the reply of one of the neighboring rabbis. "We must concentrate all our efforts on those who are devoted to the ideals of Judaism."

"Your vision is too narrow," pleaded Rabbi Kook. "*All* of the children of Israel received the Torah at Mount Sinai, not just the sons of pious scholars and leaders. We must help them to realize what a great inheritance they have. These people need our help even *more* than those who are devoted and faithful. At least the latter have their faith and knowledge to keep them loyal to the Jewish fold. Those who have gone astray are sinking deeper and deeper into a life devoid of all Jewish values."

Rabbi Kook would argue with these rabbis endlessly.

"How can you ignore the great body of Israel for a few faithful students? I agree that we must develop the young and exploit the talent and intellectual resources in our midst, but the others are also our brethren. Do they deserve our care and attention any less than the *Yeshiva Bachurim*?"

"Abraham, Abraham," they would implore him, "Why do you care for these blasphemers of the name of God? They only bring shame to the Jewish community."

Rabbi Kook felt a burning desire to prove these men

wrong. He felt that they were so engrossed in their books that they were ignorant about what was happening to the ranks of Jewry.

In order to stimulate more interest in the problems of loss of Jewish identity, Rabbi Kook decided to start a rabbinical magazine dedicated to discussing modern problems which were weakening Jewish life. The magazine was called *Ittur Sofrim* (Omissions of the Scholars).

But Abraham was still very young. When the first issue was published he was only twenty-three years old. Despite his great learning and his zeal for helping his lost brethren, his lack of experience and maturity brought his venture to failure. The first issue published was also the last.

At this point in his life, amidst despair over his rabbinical journal, another important teacher came into his life.

Rabbi Kook was told that the famous Rabbi Israel Meir of Radin was going to lecture in a nearby community on "The Evils of Gossip and Slander." Eagerly, he travelled to the lecture, and listened carefully to every word. Rabbi Israel Meir had written a book about this same subject, called *Hafetz Haim,* and, as was the custom, people called him by the name of his most famous book. He was thus known as "the Hafetz Haim."

After the lecture, Rabbi Kook came up to the Hafetz Haim and asked if he could study with him on this and other themes.

"Of course, young man. It will be a privilege to study with a young colleague with such an eager spirit."

"You know, Rabbi Israel," said Abraham, "I am a *Kohen,* just as you are, perhaps we could review together the laws of the priesthood and the sacrificial service. In this way, when the redemption comes, and the temple is restored, we will be prepared."

"I think that is an excellent idea. We can begin next week."

The two rabbis spent many hours together. For weeks and months, they reviewed the sections of the Code of Jewish Law which deal with priests and the temple worship.

After a year passed, the Hafetz Haim gave Rabbi Kook some important advice.

"Abraham, my friend," he said in a frank manner, "I think it is time for you to seek a community that needs a rabbi and to serve it. You need the practical experience of solving community problems, of helping people solve their dilemmas, and of answering questions of Jewish Law."

"But I don't want to become involved in these matters," answered Abraham. 'That will take too much time from my studies."

"Just to sit by yourself and study, or even to help another rabbi on occasion, will not suffice. To really fulfill God's will, one must be of service to his fellow man."

Abraham began to see the logic in the words of the elderly rabbi. After a long discussion and much thought, he finally accepted the idea.

OFF TO ZOIMEL

Thus, at age twenty-four, Abraham became the rabbi of a small town called Zoimel.

The six years he spent there were quiet years, and although there was not as much activity as he had expected, it was still a good opportunity to get to know the problems of a Jewish community and try to solve them. He also continued with his studies, and by the end of his sixth year in Zoimel he achieved much wisdom and maturity.

One of the problems that he encountered in Zoimel was that many people were not careful to observe all of the ritual commandments of the Jewish religion. One of the extremely important rituals which he saw was being neglected – was the wearing of *tefilin* (phylacteries). *Tefilin* are two small black boxes containing quotations from the Bible, which are wrapped around the head and arm during the daily morning worship, except on the Sabbath and holidays.

Rabbi Kook taught the people about the background of *tefilin*, and coaxed them with all his energy to restore the ritual. Finally, he decided to compose a book, compiling everything he taught about the *tefilin*. This was his first book. He did not sign his name to it because he did not want credit or glory. All he wanted was that people observe the ritual in their morning prayers. He distributed it free of charge to all the people of the town, hoping to reach them through the book as well as personal contact.

Once, while Rabbi Kook served in Zoimel, an epidemic of cholera broke out. Many died from its ravaging influence, and scores of others lay ill. When Yom Kippur arrived that year, Rabbi Kook knew that if his community would fast as prescribed by the Torah, it would only worsen their state of weakness.

To prevent this, he did a daring and courageous thing. On Yom Kippur morning he stepped up to the *Bimah* (pulpit) of the synagogue with a piece of bread in his hand, pronounced the blessing over bread, and proceeded to eat it in front of the entire congregation.

Needless to say, the people were shocked. On the most sacred day of the Jewish year, the community Rabbi was violating the obligation to fast!

"God gave us His law," explained Rabbi Kook, "so that we may live by it, not die by it." He was quoting a Talmudic dictum, based on the Bible. "It is much more important," he continued to explain, "to obey the laws of guarding one's health than to fulfill a ritual commandment. We must all eat to preserve our strength and our health. Thus, we will live to fast on many more Yom Kippurs in the future."

The people realized that Rabbi Kook was steeped in Jewish law, and knew whereof he spoke. They then joined him in a light meal to preserve their health.

Finally, Rabbi Kook felt himself ready to become a religious leader in a larger town. He was now thirty years old. When an invitation came to him one day to become rabbi of the large city of Boisk, in Latvia, he gladly accepted. This was to be a new and important challenge in his life.

6

MEDIATOR IN A FIERCE BATTLE

Rabbi Kook moved from the small, quiet village of Zoimel to the large, busy metropolis that was Boisk, a city filled with controversy and bitterness among the Jewish leaders and the masses.

Upon arrival in Boisk, he wasted no time in plunging into the arena of debate between two opposing forces – the religious and secular Zionists.

A word of background is in order here.

For a brief while in Russia, beginning in 1865, Czar Alexander II attempted to assimilate the Jewish population with the rest of the people. He freed them from their ghettos, opened certain once-closed business opportunities to them, and gave them the chance to be like other Russians.

The plan did not last long. After only a few years, an attitude of anti-Semitism again swept across Russia. While the plan lasted, many young Jews took advantage of studies outside the realm of Judaism. The study of Talmud and Torah were replaced by the study of science, mathematics, literature, music, and art.

It was only natural that given a taste of long-suppressed

freedom these people were drawn from the ghettos and attracted to the secular world. Soon, their love for learning and study was transferred from Jewish studies to European culture.

Along with the new learning came new ideas which intruded on their religious beliefs and weakened their practice of the old traditions. The Yeshivot and study halls were practically deserted, while the universities swarmed with Jews. The four wallsof the ghetto community, the confinement to a strictly Jewish residential area, became a thing of the past. Modernity set in quickly and decisively with the young Jewish intellectuals.

This movement to acquire knowledge besides that of Judaism was part of an ideology known as "Haskala," (enlightenment) which had already begun in western Europe during the eighteenth century.

Now Haskala was spreading to eastern Europe. But its reputation had preceded it, and the religious Jews of eastern Europe had already seen and heard of the results of this new movement.

Upon his arrival in Boisk, Rabbi Kook made the acquaintance of many of the leading rabbis. To determine the state of the community, he would have long discussions with them to keep himself informed of all he had to know in his position as a spiritual leader in the community.

He was warned by many people. "Be very careful of the *Maskilim* (those who were part of the Haskala movement)," said one rabbi. "They have strayed so far from their ancestral traditions that many of them completely denounce their Jewish ties, and have become either non-believers or Christians. This is part of their program to be accepted by the 'outside world.' "

Rabbi Kook took heed of the warning, but also was determined to examine the situation himself, and make his own judgments.

"Look what happened to the Mendelssohns," said one rabbi in anger. He was referring to one of the founders of the Haskala movement, Moses Mendelssohn (1729-1786). Mendelssohn translated the Bible from Hebrew into German and immersed himself in European learning, all in an attempt to spread secular knowledge among his fellow Jews and "enlighten" their minds with Western culture. His son converted to Christianity and his grandson, Felix, the famous musician, was raised as a Christian, knowing nothing of his Jewish background.

"We must not let the tentacles of the Haskala monster reach any further into our territory," the rabbis argued. They then tried to convince Rabbi Kook to help them fight the *Maskilim*. "They are nothing more than Satan in disguise," they declared.

Rabbi Kook spent part of his first few weeks in Boisk visiting some of the *Maskilim*. They, too, explained their position to him.

"For us," they said in honesty, "a university education is a 'must' for all people, Jews and non-Jews. In observing the narrowness of the education of our fathers, we have stepped briskly into the modern world and have rejected the old ways."

"Yes," agreed Rabbi Kook, "but you have deserted a way of life that has been preserved for thousands of years!"

"It is not our intention," they answered in defense of their movement, "to move completely away from Judaism. We have retained the elements of Jewish tradition which help us maintain our Jewish identification, and removed the element of religious ritual. We cannot accept what seems to us as outmoded beliefs and ritual practices. We have a great deal of group pride and loyalty, and want very much to remain Jews. We want to be Jews in our home, and men on the street."

"Don't you see," said Rabbi Kook, "that inevitably this

results in your becoming men of totally secular culture, without retaining much of Jewish flavor in your lives? All you have in common with other Jews is a feeling of wanting to be a member. But you have no meaningful traditions to bind you with the rest of world Jewry.

"This isn't entirely true," answered one of the *Maskilim*. "We have our participation in the Zionist Movement. This will enable us to express our group loyalty, our love for the Homeland, and our national language. In short, we give creative expression to our feeling for Jewishness without accepting all of the trappings of Jewish religion which are repugnant to us."

Rabbi Kook found himself between the anvil and the hammer. His feelings could be expressed in the words of Shakespeare: "A curse on both your houses." He felt that both sides had gone too far and that it was his task to bring both sides to see their mistakes.

Being a deeply pious and meticulously observant Jew, his religious life was certainly more closely aligned with that of the Orthodox Jews than any other group. Yet, his training under tolerant and open-minded teachers like Rabbi Berlin, made him sympathize with the *Maskilim* as well.

He felt the rabbis went too far in their denunciation of the Maskilim, and he told them so.

"Do not think," he said, "that what happened to Mendelssohn's family will necessarily happen to everybody espousing the cause of the Haskala. It is true that some of our people drank so heavily at the well of secular books that they drowned their Jewish background, but this does not necessarily mean that their original intention was what caused the end of their Judaism."

The reason Rabbi Kook could achieve some success with his rabbinical colleagues, as a mediator, was because the pious rabbis all looked to him as a leader and guide. His learning was deep. His love of God and zealous devotion to

Judaism was beyond reproach. It was impossible to charge that his motives were to lead Jews away from their religion. People were forced to listen to him and take his words seriously because of the high position he enjoyed in the Jewish community.

Besides being merely tolerant of Jewish nationalism, and passively accepting the Zionist cause, he saw it as a way to hasten the coming of the Messiah. But his colleagues did not agree.

"You are not hastening the coming of the Messiah," argued one rabbi in Boisk. "What this new national feeling is doing is *replacing* the Messiah!"

After living in Boisk for some time, and trying to heal the vast rift between the two segments of the community, he consolidated his feelings into an article that was published in a scholarly magazine, entitled: "The Mission of Israel and Its Nationhood."

In the essay, Rabbi Kook wrote that Jewish nationalism, far from being anti-Jewish, was part of God's plan for the universe. God implanted into the hearts of Jews a love for their people. Even when their faith waivered, their loyalty to their fellow Jews would bind them together until such time as would permit revitalization of their faith.

Those who could not for the moment accept Hebrew as "Leshon Ha-Kodesh," the holy tongue, would at least revive it as the folk language. Those who did not believe that God gave Abraham and his descendents Eretz Yisrael as an eternal inheritance, at least saw the land as a place of refuge where they could establish political independence and live a free community life. Those who did not believe that God, in His love for Israel, ordained commandments and observances, would perpetuate the customs as folk-ways and part of their national, if not religious, life.

By seeing the mission of Zionism as part of the Divine Plan, Rabbi Kook was able to help other orthodox people accept this great and important movement and make it the ultimate aim of orthodox and non-orthodox alike.

It was at this junction in his life that Rabbi Kook began to develop his overall view of Jewish philosophy and Jewish living. He felt a deep and strong love for all Jews, and wanted to see them united as one people. He hoped that they would eventually express their commitment to God and His Torah, in unity.

The other rabbis would often criticize anyone who had a secular (general, non-religious) education. "They are neglecting the Torah and relying on vain knowledge," they would say.

Rabbi Kook disagreed. "I see no danger in any kind of learning, as long as it is accompanied by Jewish learning. I have a deep faith in the Torah's ability to stand for itself in competition with the wisdon of other peoples."

Rabbi Kook had read the works of the philosophers of many nations, and was influenced by them in his thinking. "So long as books help one understand the universe, they are acceptable and helpful."

He felt that knowing other fields of inquiry not only did not prevent one from being religious, but it sometimes helped one become even more religious. "Mathematics, science, and the study of nature, are all legitimate means of achieving awareness of God's marvelous creations. But they must be accompanied by a knowledge of the Torah, for this was our great contribution to the world. It is the sacred books which give purpose and direction to the contents of the other books. Study of the Torah adds the dimension of holiness to one's life and illuminates other areas of study. No other books can do that for our people."

With this new philosophy, summarized in the article he wrote as Rabbi of Boisk, he began to win adherents to *religious* Zionism. Thus, he met the challenge of modernism head-on by adapting the new to the old and helping infuse new life into old forms. In this way, he helped Jewish life be more creative and dynamic, and less stagnant and congealed.

His article was read by students at the Yeshivot and by rabbis all over eastern Europe. His name and his ideas began to spread among Jewry, worldwide.

Only one year after its publication, religious Zionists joined together to form a movement still active today, the Mizrachi Zionist Organization. At the founding convention, one of the leaders announced: "The article on Zionism by Rabbi Abraham Isaac Kook will act as the basis for the philosophy of our new organization."

"We must all recognize," proclaimed another speaker from the convention platform, "that as Rabbi Kook has taught, Zion and Torah are two sanctities that supplement and imply one another."

With this success behind him, Rabbi Kook began to receive invitations from large communities all over Russia and eastern Europe to become their Rabbi. But he had something else in mind, something he had been dreaming about for a long, long time. His next change of location would be dramatically different from any of the previous ones.

7

HOME, AT LAST

One Sabbath morning after services, Rabbi Kook announced to the congregation of worshippers in the Boisk synagogue that he would be leaving them soon.

"I have decided," he said with a feeling mixed with joy and sadness, "to fulfill the commandment I have been longing to perform since I was a small child. I want to go to Eretz Yisrael."

The reaction of the congregation was of shock and dismay. "How can you leave Russia, where hundreds of thousands of Jews need your spiritual guidance? In Palestine there is only a handful of settlers. You must stay where you are needed."

The argument was compelling. A shepherd must remain where his flock is, regardless of adverse circumstances. He cannot desert them for his own shelter or safety. Perhaps Rabbi Kook was acting selfishly in making this decision. But only the future would tell.

Trying to defend himself, he told his friends the following: "I am now thirty-nine years old. If I postpone this lifelong dream any longer, I know it will be too late. While I still have the strength to change my way of life, I must move to the land of my ancestors and settle there. In another five or ten years I will be almost fifty, and then it will be too late."

"But what will you gain?" they persisted. "There is hardly a *minyan* (quorum) of Jews to attend synagogue services in the city you want to go to." (Rabbi Kook had chosen the city of Jaffa for his first residence in Eretz Yisrael, where only a small Jewish community lived). "You will meet only the *Maskilim*, who have recently gone there. They will only mock you, and we here who yearn for your spiritual leadership will be without it."

Still the rabbi remained firm. He knew that his father-in-law, Rabbi Elijah David Rabinowitz-Tomin had already migrated to Palestine and was now Chief Rabbi of the city of Jerusalem. He, too, wanted to be among those who dared to "go up."

"We will increase your salary; we will pay all of your debts; we will do anything," the people of Boisk pleaded with him again and again. Rabbi Kook remained adamant.

Finally, the congregation wrote to the Jews of Jaffa and told them they would prevent their rabbi from leaving the city because he had too many debts. But the answer came back that the people of Jaffa had already sent Rabbi Kook enough money to meet all of his financial obligations.

The moment could be postponed no longer. Rabbi Kook and his family gathered their belongings, boarded the boat, and waved good-bye to their many dear friends. At last, he was going home.

IN JAFFA

As the boat approached the Jaffa harbor, Rabbi Kook watched the rounded coast line, behind which stood Arab buildings with minarets at the top. Quaint colors and designs suggested the Semitic background of its inhabitants. People in poorly-made clothing scurried about in the market place just beyond the beach. The day was clear, and the sun lit up the Holy Land with its dazzling rays.

Rabbi Kook's heart was filled with gratitude and joy that God had permitted him to live to experience this great occasion. As the boat knocked against the docks, he pronounced the ancient blessing, the *She-he-cheyanu:* "Blessed art Thou, O Lord our God, King of the Universe, Who hast preserved us, and has kept us in life, and enabled us to reach this occasion."

As soon as he stepped off the boat onto the holy soil itself, he bent down, fell on his face, and kissed the soil he had longed to touch for so many, many years.

It is told that the first time Rabbi Kook saw a cow in Palestine, he ran over to it, kissed it and exclaimed exuberantly, "Oh! a real, live, Eretz-Yisrael cow!"

To him, this was not like arriving in a foreign country, even though he had never before set foot on its ground. It was more like coming home after a long, involuntary and roundabout journey. He was like a traveller, weary of being away, yearning for the comforts of home. But he knew that the comforts which were waiting for him in this new homeland were not material.

He had no house, no possessions. No loved ones and friends were waiting to welcome him back. All he had was the knowledge that a life-long dream was finally coming into fruition. All he had was the knowledge that he would soon walk on the soil that was trod by Samuel, Elijah, Amos, and Isaiah, the great prophets and leaders of Israel.

In some ways he was a stranger. In many more ways, he was a native. He knew its long and colorful history. He was familiar with its national tongue. The experience moved him deeply, almost like a child taking his first trip out of the city. From the moment he first stepped off the boat, he knew that his choice to come to Eretz Yisrael was the only one he could have made.

But all was not as easy as it seemed the first few days off the boat. The problems which would face him in the very near future were numerous.

8

FACING PROBLEMS IN JAFFA

After acting as mediator in many community battles in the Diaspora, Rabbi Kook expected things to be serene and uncomplicated in Eretz Yisrael. He looked forward to harmony and peace in the Holy Land.

He could not have been farther from right. The conflicts he knew in the Old World were like petty quarrels compared to the new ones he would encounter.

His father-in-law, Rabbi Tomim, then chief rabbi of Jerusalem, came to have dinner at the Kook home shortly after the arrival of his daughter and son-in-law.

"Things here in Eretz Yisrael will not be easy," he cautioned him. "People here hold strong personal opinions, which, by the way, they do not hesitate to voice very vehemently."

"I have never hid my face from problems, Father, you know that," said Abraham.

"Yes, Abraham, but these are different and more difficult problems. In the first place, there are different communities of Jews here - from different parts of the world. There are Jews from the eastern countries who speak Arabic, the Sephardic Jews, and then there are Jews from western Europe, who speak Yiddish, the Ashkenazic Jews."

"All that is true, Father, but now they are living together and things will definitely change."

"Do not minimize these differences in background, Abraham, because these immigrants have brought with them their age-old rivalry for prominence and prestige. Each community maintains its own school system, its own legal apparatus, its own rabbis, and its own functionaries." (Even to this day, the State of Israel has one Chief Rabbi for the Sephardic Jews, and one for the Ashkenazic Jews.)

"Each community," continued Rabbi Tomim, "brought its own pronunciation of Hebrew, and its own variations of synagogue ritual and liturgy. Sometimes these differences become irreconcilable."

"Then I must work with one group at a time until I can get them to trust each other," insisted Abraham.

"You will still have problems," added his father-in-law. "Even among the Ashkenazic Jews there are differences. You know yourself that your own family was divided between Hasidim and Mitnagdim. The Hasidim lay emphasis upon joy and music and dance to accompany their prayers and religious celebrations. The Mitnagdim stress learning and sobriety."

"I am beginning to see what you mean," answered the younger rabbi, as he became more aware of what he was soon to face. "I can even add another difference to those you have mentioned. I know, for example, that there are people here who have been here for decades, living from *halukah*, the charity of world Jewry. Then there are newcomers, the pioneers who pride themselves on not taking handouts, but on making their own success."

"Right you are, my son. All of these differences only serve to drive wedges between the settlers in the Holy Land."

Rabbi Kook saw that his work was indeed going to be

important and difficult. Once again, he would be called upon to serve as a conciliator to negotiate, to appease, to pacify, and to cement friendly relations between the old and the new, the traditional and the modern, the Easterner and Westerner, the pious and the rebellious.

The first thing he did after getting settled in Jaffa, only two weeks after his arrival, was to make a tour of all the colonies where Jews lived.

In each place he visited, his presence was always welcomed with joy and appreciation. In the vineyards and on orange fields, people gathered to see the new rabbi of Jaffa and its surrounding communities. The fact that he made the effort to come see them and their progress was enough to boost their morale.

"What can I do to help you?" he asked in each place he stopped. "What problems are you facing? Perhaps I can suggest a solution."

Usually the answer came back, "We have no weddings or circumcision ceremonies to arrange, Rabbi. We really do not need your help, but thank you for offering."

"What do you mean, weddings? I meant financial help, or advice for your personal problems. Please let me help you in any way you need my services."

For the first time, these young people, many of whom were university graduates, were able to speak to a bearded, eastern European rabbi, who spoke to them on their own level and who showed sympathy for their ideals and interests. He did not come to criticize or to chastise them, only to help.

After a hard day's work on the farm, the colony members would sit around tables drinking tea. Rabbi Kook would often join them and chat with them. They discussed anything from tomato growing to Marxist Socialism.

"Are you sure you are a rabbi and not a professor in disguise?" they often asked. "How can you know so much about so many things – agriculture, philosophy, economics, and at the same time be an expert in Jewish matters?" Their respect for him grew enormously after such conversations, which often lasted long into the night.

Little by little, he was able to win their confidence. As his reputation spread, he began to receive invitations to make public addresses so that many could come together and hear his unique views on modern Jewish problems. Thus, long after his arrival he agreed to deliver his first lectures to the Jaffa and surrounding communities.

Many questions lay in the hearts of the people. "What would the rabbi speak about in his first talk? How would he address himself to so many different kinds of people? What language would he use?"

When the evening for his lecture arrived, he rose to the improvised platform that had been prepared for him, and began to speak.

"Why, it's Hebrew that he's speaking," one whispered to the other. "A traditional rabbi is speaking in the Holy Tongue. He is like one of us, yearning to renew the Hebrew language, not spoken by the masses for two thousand years."

The effect on the people was enormous. To the young intellectuals, who saw Hebrew as the foundation of the new society they were striving to build, it was a great spiritual and psychological boost in morale.

Since the talk contained many quotations from the sacred books of Judaism, and since Rabbi Kook's goals, as outlined in the talk, were consistent with traditional Judaism, the traditionally-minded people in the audience were also pleased.

"This rabbi must be a very great scholar," said one to the other. "He knows so many different parts of the Talmud, and can put them together with the skill of a great orator. His erudition and piety and his fervor for our religion will go a long way in restoring our ancient values to the new settlers."

Once again, Rabbi Kook showed himself to be an adept

diplomat. He tried to please all elements, without compromising his high standards.

Several weeks before the festival of Sukkot, the Fall fruit harvest celebration, Rabbi Kook investigated plans for supplying *etrogim* to the community; that is, the yellow, lemon-like citrus fruit which is used during the Festival ritual.

"Where do we receive our *etrogim?*" he asked the head of one of the farm colonies.

"We get beautiful ones from the Greek island of Korfu," he answered. "They supply them to Jews in many parts of the world."

An idea struck Rabbi Kook.

"Why can't we grow them here in Eretz Yisrael? After all, during the harvest festival we are celebrating the harvest of our own crops in Eretz Yisrael. It is only natural that we use *etrogim* from the Holy Soil itself. In that way we can grow them and sell them to Jews everywhere, and help support our fellow Jews here working on the farms."

"That is an excellent idea," responded the farmer. "It certainly would be a boost to our economy. We have such a hard time eking out our living here during these pioneering days of settlement."

Rabbi Kook was happy that his suggestion was well received. "I will immediately dispatch letters to rabbis in communities all over Europe and Palestine," he said. "They must buy *etrogim* next year from the soil of Eretz Yisrael!"

The impact this action had on the settlers was hard to describe. They were thrilled that their rabbi had such a deep concern for their material welfare.

When the project of producing *etrogim* worked out well, he suggested further that more wine be produced and sold to Jewish communities throughout the world. Again, he sent letters to scores of rabbis, asking their help in promoting sale of wine from Eretz Yisrael.

"Both for ritual and general purposes," he wrote, "you

should buy only wine from our cellars here in Palestine."

By these actions, he earned the title of "godfather of the colonies." He showed that he was indeed a shepherd of his flock, ministering to all their needs. All of the predictions in Boisk that the heretics of Palestine would reject this pious rabbi, turned out to be untrue. On the contrary, they welcomed him with open arms.

"After all," he wrote one of his former friends in Boisk, "these people are dedicated workers, working themselves to the bone to eke out a meager existence from the soil, striving to build a new and creative nation. I am helping them only because I love them. And, if they love me in return, it is only because we are here in the peaceful and harmonious atmosphere of Eretz Yisrael."

Despite the time he spent in providing personal and economic advice, Rabbi Kook did not cease giving his daily lectures at the Yeshiva. In the academy of Jaffa, he saw a chance to raise a generation of rabbinic disciples who would know tradition, and yet be sensitive to the needs of the masses.

In addition to the Yeshiva, he helped found and establish high schools and vocational schools.

Once, when he visited a group of teenage Talmud students who were sitting and studying with a teacher, he asked them what trade or profession they would like to learn to support themselves.

"We do not need a trade," came the unexpected answer. "Don't you know about *Haluka*? It's the charity we get from abroad. We will study all our lives and they will support us."

"Why will you not learn a trade and find your own support?" he asked them. "Why should you be dependent on others for your sustenance? Everyone must know a trade. This is even commanded by the Mishna."

Some students were convinced that they should stop spending *all* of their time on their religious studies, and reserve at least a small portion of their schedule to prepare for their future. In the schools which Rabbi Kook helped found, there were facilities for them to learn vocations which gave them new respect for themselves and new confidence in their future. They no longer had to rely on charity from abroad.

RABBI KOOK'S FAME SPREADS

Within a year of his arrival, Rabbi Kook's reputation had begun to spread throughout the entire *Yishuv* (Jewish settlement in the Holy Land). Individuals wrote to him with all types of problems.

One letter he received read as follows:

Dear Rabbi:

My son seems to be drifting away from the ways of our ancestors. His views about God and Torah are heresy. Shall I beat him, or merely send him from our household and not permit him to return until he changes his mind? I cannot control him any longer."

"A son," responded the rabbi, "should be loved for what he is, and not for what he believes. It is merely part of his youthful idealism that makes him want to espouse new causes. Beware of judging him too harshly. We are living in troubled times. Be kind and gentle, and give him much love. God will show him the right path in good time."

To other parents, writing with similar problems, he wrote, "Try to stress the nationalistic aspects of Jewish life and attempt to instill into your children a love for the people of Israel. This in itself will mean a great deal. Through love for his people the young person will come to be reunited with his heritage."

"Doubt," he wrote to another correspondent, "is a natural and healthy part of learning. In fact, doubt is God's method of testing one's faith. Only after doubts arise and have been resolved can there emerge a really strong faith."

If a tolerant and sympathetic man like Rabbi Abraham Isaac Hakohen Kook could enter into a public battle with someone, we can be assured that the reasons were good. In the case of his battles with Eliezer Ben-Yehuda there was ample justification. This was the next major episode in his conflict-filled life.

9

CLASH WITH BEN-YEHUDA

Eliezer Ben-Yehuda was a frail, tubercular, scholarly-looking man who came to settle in Palestina from Lithuania in 1881. He was obsessed with the idea of reviving the Hebrew language, and with it, the Jewish national home.

But in his zeal for national revival, Ben-Yehuda left no room for any religious element in his new life. He was, at one point, one of the loudest opponents of the old ways of Jewish life. This was ironic for a man who almost single-handedly revived the ancestral language among the people.

After being in Palestine only one year, Rabbi Kook found himself in open conflict with Ben-Yehuda.

Ben-Yehuda was not pleased with conditions in the Holy Land and began having doubts about making Palestine the seat of the new Jewish Nation. Once, he argued with Rabbi Kook about it.

"How can we live among hostile people?" he asked the rabbi. "Palestine is now in the hands of an unfriendly nation, Turkey. It is not the logical place, therefore, for a Hebraic revival. I think a place like Uganda, the African territory offered by the British to Theodore Herzl, would suit our needs better."

Rabbi Kook was astounded. "How can any Jewish national revival occur in a land other that Eretz Yisrael? It is inconceivable!"

"You argue this way," said Ben-Yehuda, "because you are unavoidably tied to the past. It is time you released yourself from the chains of tradition and accepted reality. How can we live in peace among the Turks?"

Rabbi Kook became angry. "The land is so closely tied to our people that Uganda could not possibly arouse the burning enthusiasm needed to revive a Jewish national state! Only Eretz Yisrael, the land of the patriarchs and the prophets and Kings, can do this for us!"

When the debate became too heated, Rabbi Kook arose and left.

A short time later, Rabbi Kook read an article in a local newspaper, written by Ben-Yehuda, which called orthodox Jews "ancestor-worshippers." He even went so far as to say that he was glad to see the young generation "turning its back upon our past – this is our pride."

When Rabbi Kook read this, his anger was aroused even more. He sat down and wrote a lengthy letter expressing his views of Ben-Yehuda's attitude towards the past and towards tradition. Then he called over his secretary.

"I want this letter circulated," he told her, "among all the colonists. We must condemn this negative way of thinking. Why don't these irreligious nationalists realize that even for them it is only the historic associations of the past that can bind our people to their homeland. Even *they* cannot sever their connections with their memories, or they are doomed. "Jews, God, Torah, and Eretz Yisrael are all one," he said. "To separate any of them is like removing a limb from a body."

Then he turned to a friend sitting on the other side of his office. "By condemning the Jewish past, people like Ben-

Yehuda are joining hands with those who would villify the good name of our people. Many are the anti-Semites who desecrate our history and challenge our historic contributions to mankind. Why give them strength from our own ranks?"

But Rabbi Kook not only scolded Ben-Yehuda for his misguided ideas, he also placed part of the blame for the existence of such heresy on the shoulders of the rabbis themselves.

In his circular letter, he wrote: "How can we expect people to respect our past if their own rabbis don't help keep it alive? If those who stand at the helm of the Jewish ship do not guide it into new and fresh waters, it will crash upon the rocks of indifference and boredom."

Kook charged the contemporary rabbis in Palestine and elsewhere with being lazy and lacking proper perspective.

"It is our duty," he wrote in the same letter, "to work *with* the living and *for* the living in order to sanctify life. You who sit all day and bury your noses only in your books, are not truly fulfilling God's will. There is more to Jewish life than study. Study must lead to action; to good deeds."

What Rabbi Kook dreamed of seeing in his lifetime in the revived Eretz Yisrael was a continuation of the culture and religion of Judaism, not just a reliance on past laurels.

He longed to see serious attempts at new religious poetry, of which he himself wrote much, and philosophic tracts attempting to fuse Jewish thinking with the best of world ideas. His colleagues would only sit and memorize what *others* had written, without making any contributions of their own. This he saw as only half of the task of full divine service.

"Since there is a vacuum in modern literature," he wrote, "if *we* do not furnish the necessary creativity, it will be supplied by our ideological opponents, the secularists.

"One cannot sit back and scold people for not adhering to the tenets of Judaism if the teachers of the age are not ready to make these beliefs sweet in the mouth of the masses."

With these stern warnings, he chided his colleagues, and tried to goad them into action.

In 1909, he revived his former idea of publishing a journal for creative Jewish thought. He was now forty-four years old, and his influence was widespread. Unfortunately, the attempt died once again and only one issue saw the light of day, most of it written by the hand of the editor – Rabbi Kook himself. His hopes for a literary renaissance were again dashed against the rocks of lethargy and indifference on the part of his colleagues.

His own contributions to this magazine show that living in Eretz Yisrael had had a profound effect on him. His writings on the psychology of holiness and piety reflect a deep urge to achieve a mystical union with the divine. Eretz Yisrael had a transforming and uplifting effect on his life.

Many of Rabbi Kook's writings from these first years in Eretz Yisrael show that just breathing the air of the Holy Land increased his religious sensitivity. His love for prayer increased and he spent more time on the words of his prayer-book, and felt a closer relationship with the words of the Bible. His life became more and more filled with joy and light from the mystical experiences he had during contemplation and reflection of God and the universe.

As the days passed, Rabbi Kook experienced more of the warm inner feelings that come with spiritual happiness. In addition to all of the active religious, economic and community affairs in which he was involved, he was privately building for himself a deeply pious personal life. His thinking and writing and speaking were filled with awe and reverence for life and the world.

Despite his accomplishments, he did not cease to look for *new* ways to help the struggling Jewish community in Eretz Yisrael. One particular decision he made in their favor immersed him into a vicious battle with his fellow rabbis.

10

RABBI KOOK DEFIES HIS COLLEAGUES

The Bible commands that every seventh year be a Sabbatical Year, known in Hebrew as the *Shmita*. During this *Shmita* year, no work can be done on the soil – no farming whatsoever. The land must lie fallow.

In addition, in the *Shmita* year all debts are cancelled. This second requirement made it difficult in post-biblical times for people to borrow money. A lender knew that if the person to whom he lent money kept the loan past the *Shmita* year, every seventh year, he would not be able to collect the loan.

During biblical times, this was a way of preventing someone from having to sell himself into slavery to repay his debts. But in post-biblical, or Talmudic times, when the economy was based on large capital investments, this became a great problem because loans were a necessary part of business.

In the First Century, C.E., Rabbi Hillel, head of the *Sanhedrin* (Jewish legal-judicial authority), made a special enactment known as a *takkana*. This *takkana* permitted the *court* to collect the debt instead of the lender, even after the beginning of the *Shmita* year. This kept the letter of the biblical law intact, since the lender was not directly collecting his debt during the *Shmita* year. It also provided a solution to the socio-economic problem of the age.

Rabbi Hillel's *takkana* is always remembered by rabbis as an ingenious contribution to Jewish law, because it helped keep the law viable and flexible. If there were no ways to adapt the law, people would view it as too rigid and disregard it.

By making this *takkana,* Hillel was able to maintain public respect for *all* Jewish laws, not only *Shmita.*

The other stipulation of the *Shmita* year, that the land lie fallow for a whole year, had not been a question for many centuries. After the year 70 C.E., when the Romans drove the Jews out of their homeland, Jews lived in what is known as the Diaspora – countries other than Palestine – and were no longer making a living from the soil.

Beginning in the 1880's however, when Jewish people began to form agricultural colonies in the Holy Land, this question came up once more. The year 1888 was a *Shmita* year and the problem presented itself for the first time in twenty centuries.

In that year, a group of representatives from the farming community came to discuss the problem with some of the leading rabbis of the day in Palestine.

"It is very difficult for us," they explained, "even if we work very hard before the arrival of the *Shmita* year. The land has not been worked for many centuries. We are pioneers struggling to support ourselves from the soil. Observance of the *Shmita* year at this time would mean economic strangulation for many of our new farm colonies."

Some of the rabbis turned a deaf ear. But three of them listened sympathetically and established a rabbinical court to adjudicate the matter. In Jewish tradition, formal legal procedures could only be performed by a court composed of three rabbis.

"We must do something for these farmers," said one rabbi to the other two. "We cannot let them become discouraged with the rigorous laws of our faith. Here is a case in which we can follow the legal precedent of Rabbi Hillel of the ancient *Sanhedrin* and make a *takkana*."

"Some way must be found," agreed a second rabbi, "to enable them to continue tilling the soil. It is important now that the land be worked, and that it produce enough food for increasing numbers of immigrants. If we ask Jews from different parts of the world to uproot themselves to come and live here, we must be prepared to provide them with food."

"I have it," exclaimed the third rabbi. "We will make a fictional sale of the land to non-Jews. The laws of the Torah are not applicable to them. Then we can continue to work the land, because it will not, technically, be our property."

They all agreed and the *takkana* was proclaimed by the court of three rabbis. Almost immediately, opposition arose from the camp of the more traditional rabbis. One such rabbi from Jerusalem, wrote a letter to the court, protesting their action.

"You are violating the Torah," he wrote. "How can you flout God's law willfully? If we are really devoted to the law, we can find ways of obeying it. We can accept contributions of charity through the *Haluka* system from Jews in other countries."

The three rabbis answered the letter. "This would not be an adequate solution. First of all, it would not provide enough to meet all of our needs. But even more important than this, it would demoralize the young pioneers. They have come here from Russia, where they were persecuted and lived at the mercy of other people's will. Here they want to feel and act as independent, self-sustaining Jews with self respect, earning their own way. They are building a new life for themselves, and must begin rebuilding the land for many more immigrants who will follow them in the future. No, charity is not the answer."

The problem was solved for the year 1888, but what would be of the years to come?

The first *Shmita* year after Rabbi Kook's arrival in the Holy Land was *1909*. This was his first chance to deal with the problem. Knowing about the precedent of 1888, he began making plans to apply the same *takkana* to the year *1909*, and for all future *Shmita* years.

His colleagues discouraged him.

"You know, Abraham," said one rabbi, "that your own uncle, Rabbi Mordecai Gimpel Yaffe, did not accept the decision in 1888 when he was rabbi of the community of Ekron, in southern Palestine. He insisted on letting the land lie fallow, and he encouraged the people to use the time studying folios of the Talmud."

"That is true," answered Rabbi Kook. "I love my uncle very much, and have great respect for him. Besides, it certainly is an excellent opportunity for intensive study. Yet, I still feel that we would be causing undue hardship to the young colonists. I don't think God would be happy if we discouraged immigration to Eretz Yisrael at this important period of history."

"Abraham, Abraham! You know what God wants? He wants us to obey His Torah! Many great teachers of our day are *against* this *takkana*. Your very revered master, the head of the Yeshiva of Volozhin, Rabbi Berlin, is against this *takkana*. He has declared that we cannot allow financial considerations to prevent us from observing the law."

Rabbi Kook stood up and made a short statement, expressing himself with finality. "I will invite several of the leading rabbis of Eretz Yisrael to my home, and we will give vent to all of our opinions. Then I will decide how to advise the colonists who come to me."

Not long thereafter, the meeting was called and the discussion began. Rabbi Kook was almost alone in his view.

One rabbi arose from his seat and began to speak. "I must read to you this statement I found written in 1888 by one of the leading rabbis of Jerusalem: "Our Holy Torah decrees the punishment of exile from the Holy Land for disobeying the laws contained in it. How can we treat this Holy Soil which we have come to live upon in a way other than according to the plan of God?" He sat down.

A second rabbi expressed his opinion on the matter in the following way: "Gentlemen, we have a great deal at stake here. It is not only the *Shmita* year we are deciding on; it is all Jewish law relating to agriculture. If we disobey one, then we will begin to disobey all of them. For example, the Torah commands us to leave the corner of the field untouched, not to go back and pick up stray stalks and sheaves – leaving these parts for the poor to come and eat. Then, there are laws concerning farmers' contributions to the support of the Holy Temple, and to the officials of the temple – the *Kohen* and the Levite. There are also laws directing farmers to make pilgrimages to Jerusalem three times a year to observe the festivals – Passover, Shavuot, and Sukkot.

Another rabbi took his turn, basically agreeing with those who spoke before him.

"I must agree with my colleagues. We have to see this question as a part of the overall resettlement of the Holy Land. We all know that this return to Eretz Yisrael is of great significance for the Jewish people. We are all looking forward to the building here of a new, revitalized Jewish community and a restoration of all of our religious laws and their strict observance. After all, the whole purpose of the redemption is to enable Jews to perform the laws and statutes of the Torah. They are violating all of the regulations and losing the merit of holiness which the land provides to those who obey the Torah."

One by one, the rabbis in the room fought to prevent

Rabbi Kook from accepting the *takkana* and from advising the people in Jaffa and its surrounding colonies to accept it.

"Do you know," asked one rabbi in a challenging fashion, "that when you sell the Holy Land to a non-Jew, you are prohibiting our people from fulfilling the *mitzva* (commandment) of settling the land? If the land is not theirs, then they are not observing the command to come to Eretz Yisrael."

"Now you are being narrow-minded," answered Rabbi Kook. "The command to settle in the Holy Land is independent of other laws and commandments. They are still living in Eretz Yisrael, no matter whose name is on the bill of sale. We cannot be too strict in our interpretation of these matters."

"But to sell our God-given land," said another. "This is our land, given by God to Abraham and his descendants. Who are *we* to offer it for sale?"

"This sale is not a permanent, fully-binding action," answered Rabbi Kook. "It is only a paper transaction to permit us to observe God's Torah. We do the same thing on Passover when we sell the *Hametz,* or unleavened bread. (On Passover, Jews make a "paper" sale of their food and utensils to be free of all unleavened bread, as the Torah commands.) This is an old Jewish custom, and the sale is really not like an official transaction. You know that. It is merely a symbolic declaration, enabling us to avoid breaking the law."

"Oh, but Abraham," said yet another, "don't you see that you are displaying a lack of faith in God? Is it impossible for the Almighty to create a miracle and provide enough food in the sixth year for the sixth and seventh? This *is* the Holy Land, you know," he added with biting sarcasm. "By working the land during the seventh year, you are suggesting that God is not the great provider of food that we say He is in our daily prayers."

"It is certainly true," argued Rabbi Kook, "that God provides for all mankind. But the Talmud teaches us that we must not rely on miracles. We cannot expect God to serve us food all prepared on a silver tray. He provides for man through the hard labor of man himself. We are God's partners in this venture, and must do our share to sustain ourselves, without relying on miracles. Why the very fact that we are able to bring forth food from the ground altogether is a miracle."

As the hour became late, it was clear that the two sides were in a deadlock. Rabbi Kook could not be convinced to desert the pioneer colonists in their hour of great need. He felt that just as Rabbi Hillel reckoned with the social and economic conditions of his time, so must he.

Still it disturbed him that he had to permit a law of the Torah to go unobserved. He therefore suggested something to the farmers that would help them remember that it was *Shmita* year.

"Perhaps it would be wise," he suggested, "to work the land a little bit less than we would ordinarily. Perhaps we might make some marked change in our method of plowing, for example, or anything that will help us remember that this is a *Shmita* year and keep us mindful of our duties to God. Let us devote extra time for studying the Torah as we would if we were not harvesting the crops. In this way, we shall be able to preserve the spirit of the Law, and not lose sight of our general responsibilities to our religion."

Nevertheless, there were some very pious farmers who refused to accept his *takkana*. "I admire your courage in defying the opinion of so many of your fellow rabbis," said one religious farmer. "But, I feel that I cannot accept your lenient decision."

"It is not that I am courageous," answered Rabbi Kook. "I am not making this decision because I have any particular courage. The fact is that I do not have the strength to quiet my conscience which tells me what is right."

"Is it right to disobey the Torah?" asked the farmer.

"We are not disobeying the Torah," he answered. "We are merely resuming our obedience to it on a slow and gradual basis. One cannot build a new society in one day. After two thousand years of exile and persecution, how can an entire people be expected to return to their land, to rebuild it, and to perfect their spiritual, cultural and physical lives overnight? The redemption is a slow process. Some day, soon, we will be able to obey the *Shmita* laws and all the *other* laws of the Torah which we now neglect. But this will take time."

"But how long? It could be forever," challenged the farmer.

"Sometimes the will of God is fulfilled slowly. Zion will be rebuilt, the Jewish people redeemed, and a new society created of people dedicated to God and his righteous laws. But, God's ways are seen through the slow processes of nature. Great achievements do not come quickly or easily."

Despite Rabbi Kook's basic disagreement with his colleagues, he felt that they should remain friendly towards one another and united in spirit. Therefore, when two groups of rabbis threatened to make a complete break from each other, he saw this as a tragic mistake. The healing of the rift was his next project.

11

A SPLIT IN THE RANKS OF THE RABBIS

In the year 1912, a new orthodox organization appeared on the horizon of the Jewish community. It was called *Agudat Yisrael* (Society of Israel), known for short as *Agudah*. Its purpose was to foster Jewish religious life all over the world.

Rabbi Kook saw in this new organization an opportunity for the reunification of all Israel. "If only the new organization will adopt my plan and become a Zionist group, viewing Zionism as a religious movement," he felt, "it could serve as a powerful force in binding together all Jews."

Unfortunately, this was not to be the case. In fact, it turned out that the *Agudah* was anti-Zionistic. Its members were interested in fulfilling the commandment of settling in the Holy Land, but they saw no use in forcing God's hand by organizing a man-made return. God would bring the Jews back to their homeland in His own good time, they reasoned.

Being anti-Zionist, they were in direct opposition to another orthodox group already in existence: the *Mizrachi*. The *Mizrachi* was the religious wing of the World Zionist Organization.

Once, representatives of both groups came to Rabbi

Kook requesting that he affiliate with them.

"I will not join either group," he told them. "I must remain independent, so that I can help both of you see each other as you are, and perhaps help you reunite."

"But if you don't join us," said the delegation from the *Mizrachi*, "you will not be able to help further our goals. We need a man of your stature to help direct us and guide us."

Although he was very sympathetic to their cause, he remained adamant. "If I join your group, I will not be able to keep open channels of communication with the *Agudah*. There has to be someone to do this. It would be a tragic mistake if both your groups remained permanently split. It is bad enough that there is a chasm between Orthodox and Secularist. Must we make a sub-division among the Orthodox also? If Orthodoxy wishes to be influential in Jewish life, it must be united and prepared to cooperate fully on all matters."

Next, the *Agudah* group pleaded with him.

"Why won't you become a member of our Society? We need a man of your piety and learning to support our cause." He answered them in the same way. "Don't you see," he said in desparation, "that the leadership of Jewry is falling into the hands of the non-religious element? While our people are languishing in the chaos of irreligiosity, we are sitting here and quarreling among ourselves. No good can come of it!"

Still, both organizations wooed him for his support. Whoever would have the celebrated Rabbi of Jaffa on his side would gain prestige, and their cause might ultimately prevail – so they each reasoned. Rabbi Kook's true sympathies were with the *Mizrachi* side, but he withheld official affiliation in order to allow himself to remain a disinterested negotiator. Perhaps he could bring the two sides together, as he had done on so many other occasions.

On one particular occasion, the fight broke out into violent bitterness. It was 1913, just before the Eleventh World

Zionist Congress was to be held that year, in Vienna. As part of the World Zionist Organization, the *Mizrachi* group planned to send representatives to the Congress. They turned to Rabbi Kook to go and speak in their name.

"This certainly seems to me to be a splendid opportunity," he answered. "This will enable me to influence the Zionists to adopt a religious outlook. I look forward with great anticipation to this trip."

When it became known that he was planning to attend this convention, a stir was created among the people of the *Agudah*. Rabbi Kook received a letter from them a few days later.

"We beg of you," they wrote, "not to associate yourself with those non-religious Zionists of the World Zionist Organization who are building Zion without obeying the Torah. They are fostering a false notion of rebuilding the Holy Land. It can only be rebuilt together with the fulfillment of God's Laws."

Rabbi Kook rejected their plea to make him change his mind. He was determined to go. By speaking directly to the leaders of the Zionist movement from all parts of the world, he could present his views on nationalism based on religion. "Surely in this dialogue," he thought to himself, "I can show the secularists their error."

Fate was to lend aid to the *Agudah*. It was just at the time when Rabbi Kook was preparing to depart that Arab terrorists attacked the Jewish quarter of Jaffa.

"Abraham, perhaps you should not go," suggested his close friends. "People are coming here all hours of the day for financial and spiritual help. Who will help them if you are gone?"

"Yes, you are right," he admitted reluctantly, nodding his head. "My first duty is to be with my people in times of trouble. It seems that I shall have to forego this trip."

Seeing a frown of disappointment cover his face, his

friends made a suggestion. "Why don't you write a letter expressing your views? Then they can read it at the convention."

"That is a good idea," he conceded. His face was not as sad looking now. "This will perhaps accomplish the same thing."

The Rabbi sat down with pen and ink, and began to put his thoughts on paper.

"My dear colleagues, friends, lovers of Zion," he began. "I am truly sorry that I cannot tell you in person how strongly I feel about a certain idea I want to share with you. That idea is that the twin concepts of Israel, the people, and Torah, the Law and way of life, can never be separated. Those of you who see the revitalization of our people without a similar rebirth of the high values and ideals of our tradition are bearing false witness to the Jewish past.

"If you do nothing else at this meeting in Vienna, I want you to consider a phrase which you have included in your charter. This phrase says that 'Zionism has nothing to do with religion.'

"How far this is from the truth! I know that you wish to appeal to all Jews to join the Zionist movement, both the religious ones and the not-so-religious ones. But this denial of the historic connection between our people and their land can serve no good purpose.

"I firmly believe that it is God Himself Who planted within each of us a love of His people and His land. This strong national loyalty which God has given us, has enabled us to stay together and fulfill His Torah. If you are to represent all of world Jewry, you must expunge this vicious untruth from your statement of principles."

THE AGUDAH CONVENTION

The following year, when the *Agudah* was planning *its* convention, in Germany, Rabbi Kook was invited to address the delegates of this meeting, too.

He saw this, also, as a unique opportunity to express his views. Since he was forced to cancel his trip the year before to the convention of the World Zionist Organization, he wanted to make good use of this opportunity to speak before the *Agudah*.

Rabbi Kook and his wife set out on what they thought would be a short trip abroad, in June, 1914. His boat left Jaffa for Germany, and upon arrival in Germany, he received transportation to Berlin, the location of the assembly. He did not know it when he left, but he would not be able to return to the land he loved until 1919, a full five years later.

12

SAVED FROM PRISON

Only a few days after Rabbi Kook's arrival in Germany, the First World War broke out. Still being technically a Russian citizen, he was classified in Germany as an enemy alien, and was interned there.

Meanwhile, a group of rabbis were meeting in Berlin to plan the final details of the *Agudah* convention program. Suddenly, a messenger came running into the room.

"Rabbi Kook, the famous Rabbi of Jaffa, has been arrested by government authorities!" he shouted. "It seems that they are going to put him in jail! I heard about this from the manager of the hotel where Rabbi Kook is staying."

The rabbis stood up in shock. "We must do something right away," said the chairman of the meeting. "We can continue this meeting later."

Three of the leading rabbis of Berlin made an appointment immediately to see the German governmental authorities.

"Apparently, some error has been made," they pleaded with a German official. "This great and saintly man is now a resident of Palestine. He is no longer connected in any way with the Russian people. He has left his land of birth forever and has become an appointed religious official in his new country."

"Nevertheless, he is a Russian," said the German. "He is an enemy alien, and he must remain behind bars until the war is over."

"But it is not wise," argued a spokesman for the rabbis. "This man is a world renowned religious figure." He became indignant as he spoke. "People all over the world will condemn you for this horrible, cruel and unjust action."

Fortunately for Rabbi Kook, the rabbis had more patience and determination than the government representatives. With a war on their hands, they could not make a major issue of interning an innocent religious leader.

They finally permitted Rabbi Kook to book passage to Switzerland, on condition that he be out of the country within twelve hours.

With the help of some friends of the German rabbis, Rabbi Kook was able to hurry out of Germany, and arrive in Switzerland just before midnight June 15, 1914, with only a few minutes remaining to the twelve hour deadline.

The first thing he did was to go to a transportation office in Geneva and find out about transportation to Palestine.

"I will take anything," he said. My wife has agreed to travel in any type of ship in order to get back to our home. You must find us something."

"I am truly sorry, reverend sir," said the man behind the desk. "There doesn't seem to be any way to get to that part of the world now. The war has put an end to all normal means of sea travel."

Rabbi Kook went from office to office, trying to find some way of returning to Eretz Yisrael. But all his efforts were unsuccessful.

After a few weeks, he had almost no money left, and there was no way to make contact with friends or family at home.

Once again, a fellow rabbi came to his aid in an emergency. In Zurich, a leading rabbi made several attempts to get Rabbi Kook and his wife passage home, but to no avail.

"I am truly sorry," the rabbi apologized to his weary visitor, "but all means of transportation are tied up by the war effort. And even if there were a ship going in that direction, the papers that must be submitted for permission to get out of the country would take a long time and may even be rejected in the end."

"I am lost," said Rabbi Kook. "My funds are all used up, and I cannot return home."

"All is not lost,"answered the rabbi from Zurich. "There is a very pious and humble Jew living in a small town called St. Gallen, a Mr. Abraham Kimchi. I recall that once, after Mr. Kimchi had made a pilgrimage to Eretz Yisrael, he said that he met you and heard you speak. He was very much impressed by his visit with you. You may not remember him, but his meeting with you in Jaffa, even though it was very brief, made a deep impression on him. Let me contact him."

A few days later, the Swiss rabbi contacted Rabbi Kook again.

"I have just received a letter from Mr. Kimchi, addressed to you," he said. "This is what it says:

> Please, honored Rabbi, you have given me a great honor to give aid and hospitality to a *gadol be-yisrael* (a great leader in Israel). You would enable me to fulfill a great commandment of our religion if I could offer you hospitality. You are a traveller and a stranger here, and you are a great Rabbi and teacher in Israel. Please permit me to have the great Rabbi of Jaffa as my guest."

Rabbi Kook and his wife stayed with Mr. Kimchi in St. Gallen. He hoped to hear momentarily about his return trip to Palestine, but as months passed, and the war continued, he resolved to remain in "exile" until God would provide a way for him and his wife to return to the Promised Land. Perhaps the Almighty had a good reason for him to spend some time in the Diaspora. Maybe some important work had to be done for the cause of God and Judaism.

St. Gallen turned out to be a quiet town, conducive to study, meditation, and prayer. For the Rabbi from Jaffa, it turned out to be a deeply spiritual experience.

While in Switzerland, he composed some of his most moving philosophical books and essays. Although he was only to remain there just over a year, this period in his life turned out to be one of the most productive in his literary experience.

OFF TO LONDON

The year 1916 brought what Rabbi Kook had predicted would be the unfolding of God's purpose of his exile.

A letter arrived one day for Rabbi Kook from a newly formed congregation of recent immigrants in London, who were originally from eastern Europe.

> Dear Rabbi Kook:
>
> We are members of Congregation *Machzikey Ha-Dat* (Keepers of the Faith). We have just arrived in London, and have been trying to retain our way of life in our new land. Until now, we could not afford the services of a rabbi, but finally we have grown large enough for our own spiritual leader. We would be deeply honored if you could come to London and serve us as our rabbi. At least come to London and speak to our leaders, and then you can decide.

Rabbi Kook hurried to London and met with the synagogue leaders, whom he found to be sincere "Keepers of the Faith," as their name indicated. Rabbi Kook looked upon this opportunity as a great challenge, and accepted the offer.

But there was one condition he insisted upon before agreeing to accept the invitation.

"You will have to understand," he said with sorrow in his voice, "that my services will have to be looked upon as only temporary. If at any time I should find that I can get some means of transportation back to Jaffa, I must have your permission to leave and return there immediately."

As he spoke, he felt a longing to breathe the air of the Holy Land, to live once again in the land of the prophets and sages. But deep down he knew that his service to a congregation in London was a divinely caused event which would somehow, ultimately, have a good reason for occuring.

Thus, the Rabbi of Jaffa now became the Rabbi of London. But never did he give up hope of returning, at the first opportunity, to Palestine.

Though he tried to write and think and pray as he had done in Palestine, he could not do so in the same intense spirit. "I am not myself," he wrote to a friend. "My powers of thought and concentration have diminished in the exile. I must return soon to the place where I belong."

At the end of every letter, he would sign his name: "Rabbi Abraham Isaac Hakohen Kook, The Rabbi of Jaffa, and now in London."

He was soon to see, though, that his presence in London was to have great significance for Jews not only in London, but all over the world.

13

RESCUING THE JEWS OF LONDON

In London, Rabbi Kook ministered to a large congregation of several hundred families. His people were faithful, dedicated Jews, and his deep learning was a great inspiration to them.

Besides the opportunity to be shepherd to his own flock, he found occasions to lend his mighty voice and powerful pen to the good of Jews throughout London.

One morning as he was finishing breakfast, he received a telephone call from a newly arrived Russian Jew.

"Rabbi Kook," said the caller, "I represent a group of many Russian Jews who have recently arrived in London. We fled from the Czar because of the oppression of the Jewish people there, and came to England to seek refuge."

"Welcome to London," said Rabbi Kook. "Thank Heaven you were able to arrive here safely. How can I help you, my friend?"

"We have encountered a serious threat to our living here. Many of our group did not serve in the Army in Russia, and since England and Russia are allies, the British Government wants to return us to Russia so that we can fulfill our military obligation. They do not realize the hardships we have to endure there. What's worse, we will also have to face severe punishment for evading military service and fleeing to England, if we were to return."

"I will see what I can do," replied the rabbi. "Give me the names of the people, and their present addresses. . . ."

That same day, Rabbi Kook presented himself to the office of the Foreign Secretary of the British Government.

After waiting ten or fifteen minutes in the waiting room, he began to suspect that the secretary in the outer office was deliberately making him wait in order to discourage him from making his plea.

Briskly, he arose and walked into the office. The official, seeing how determined the rabbi was to see him, let him sit down and speak.

"I am Rabbi Kook of Congregation *Machzikey Ha-Dat,* and I came to see you on an extremely urgent matter."

"Yes, sir. Very nice of you to drop in. What can I do for you, dear Rabbi?" answered the official.

"Do you know the Bible?" asked Rabbi Kook.

"Yes, very well," came the answer. "What intelligent Englishman has neglected the great Book of Books in his education? I know the Bible and love it."

"Good," said Rabbi Kook, with a pleased grin on his face. "Then you are familiar with chapter twenty-three of Deuteronomy."

"Why, I, eh, think so," responded the official, hesitantly.

"That is the passage," continued the rabbi, "which says the following: 'You shall not give up to his master a slave who has escaped from his master to you. He shall dwell with you in your midst, in the place he shall choose within one of your towns, where it pleases him best; you shall not oppress him.' "

"A very humane law, isn't it, Rabbi," responded the Englishman.

"Humane indeed, dear sir. Then why is your government not abiding by it?"

The official suddenly lost his smile and seized the sides of his chair for support.

"What do you mean? Not *my* government, surely!"

Rabbi Kook then explained the matter of the Jewish refugees who had fled from the Czar. After having declared the biblical law "humane" voluntarily, the official could do nothing but act upon Rabbi Kook's plea at once, and the matter was closed. The Jews would remain in England.

TO JAIL WITH RABBI KOOK

With that problem solved, a second one presented itself almost immediately. It also had to do with military service. This time it involved young Jewish men who were being called into the British Army to help fight in the war.

"We want to continue our Talmudic studies," said one student to Rabbi Kook. "If we serve in the military now, we will lose several years, during which we might be able to become very learned in Jewish law and lore."

"I agree," answered the rabbi. "There certainly are enough people to fight the war without taking students of the Law. And besides, we must think of the future, after the war is over. We will have to have spiritual leaders to guide our people and teach them. Those studying now will be the future rabbis and teachers of British Jews."

"How can we convince the government of this, Rabbi," asked a second student.

"I have an idea, young men," answered Rabbi Kook, as he scratched his head and began to formulate a plan of action. "I will give you your rabbinical ordination now, presuming that you will finish your studies later. Then you will be full-fledged rabbis who cannot be taken into military service."

Suddenly, dozens of newly ordained rabbis appeared on the rolls of the British government's population census. The government began to wonder what was happening, and they traced the sudden abundance of ordinations to Rabbi Kook.

One evening, Rabbi Kook heard a knock at his door. Answering it, he saw a tall man with a brown raincoat, who reached into his pocket, took out his wallet, and showed his identification card.

"British Military Selection Board," he announced in a stern voice. "Bristol's the name. May I come in?"

"Please do. Won't you sit down?" replied the rabbi more hospitably than the man expected.

"Dear sir," said Mr. Bristol, "I know your motives are worthy, but, nevertheless, by giving out so many 'ordinations', you are reducing the size of His Majesty's Army, and letting some young men get away without doing their time in the service. We cannot permit this to continue."

"Mr. Bristol," began Rabbi Kook, "you must admit that the spiritual life of this nation is as important as its military strength. These young spiritual leaders will help strengthen the moral fiber of the country."

"Rabbi Kook, you seem to miss the point. We need more men to serve in the Army. I must put it to you very bluntly. Either you stop giving out your 'ordinations,' or we will see to it that you are prosecuted by His Majesty's Government."

With this curt warning, Mr. Bristol rose and left.

When the story about the visit was told to Rabbi Kook's students, they urged him not to endanger himself any more. They would rather serve than bring him any harm.

"No,"said Rabbi Kook to the young men, "I must show these people that the preservation of our religion is a cardinal duty among our people, and that without it we have no use for life. They will then let me retain you here."

When the government noticed that the increase in rabbinical ordinations did not cease, they sent a summons to Rabbi Kook to report to the war office.

"Please report," said the notice, "to Room 434, at 29 Trilby Square, London, at nine o'clock in the morning, the Seventeenth of November, 1917."

In room 434 sat a stern-looking gentleman in a gray tweed suit, thumbing through some papers as Rabbi Kook walked in.

After a few minutes of polite conversation, the official became serious.

"Don't you realize that your actions in ordaining so many men is liable to jeopardize your position in this country? Obviously not all of the men have completed their studies so quickly, and probably some of them do not even plan to become practicing rabbis."

"I am a man who does what he thinks is right," answered the rabbi, "regardless of the consequences. I am more concerned with the Judge in Heaven than I am with any judge on earth."

"Be warned, then, sir, that this is your last chance. Next time you will have to explain your position to a royal court."

But Rabbi Kook continued to ordain young men as rabbis despite these threats. Apparently, his determination and sincerity were enough to prevent the government from prosecuting him. Whatever the reason, he never heard another word about it. Once again he had bravely solved a problem facing his people, and turned their lives from anguish to joy.

14

GOD'S PURPOSE IS REVEALED IN LONDON

The international events which took place during World War One had a great effect on the future of the Zionist movement, and Rabbi Kook, being in London during the latter part of the war, had a great deal to do with its future plans.

Until the war, Palestine had been in the hands of the Turks, who were hostile to Jewish hopes of reoccupying the territory for the establishment of an independent Jewish State. Turkey was on the side of Germany, against the allied powers of England, Russia and, later, the United States. But as the war drew to an end, British forces were gaining on the Turks and it became more and more probable that His Majesty's government would be the next to decide the fate of the Holy Land and, therefore, the fate of the Zionist movement.

Thus, several Zionist leaders in London took advantage of the opportunity and started negotiations with the British government in an attempt to win them to their side. One of these people was a British scientist, born in Russia, named Chaim Weizmann. Dr. Weizmann was able to provide the British War Office with a vital ingredient for an effective explosive, "cordite." For this contribution, Weizmann received a large cash award, plus the friendship of many leading British officials.

Chaim Weizmann ultimately became the first President of the State of Israel when independence was declared in 1948. His dynamic personality, as well as his scientific genius, were recognized throughout the upper echelons of the British government.

Weizmann's goal was to have the British authorities issue a statement of declaration to the Zionist cause, saying that they would support a Jewish national homeland in Palestine.

In September, 1917, Dr. Weizmann was on the verge of obtaining this long-sought-for declaration. He discussed it with the Foreign Secretary, Lord Arthur James Balfour.

"I am in basic agreement with your plan Dr. Weizmann," said Lord Balfour. "But there is one great obstacle standing in the way of making such a declaration."

"Tell me what it is," answered Weizmann, "and I will try to overcome it."

"The obstacle," continued Lord Balfour, hesitantly, "is a member of your own faith who objects to the declaration."

"Who could this be?" asked Weizmann, startled. "A Jew who does not want the Jews to have Palestine for a Jewish state?"

"Yes, a Jew. And you know him very well. He is Lord Edwin Montague, Secretary of State for India, and the only Jewish member of the British Cabinet. Lord Montague is a bitter anti-Zionist."

"But why should he be antagonistic toward our cause? I cannot understand it!" Dr. Weizmann sat in his chair in disbelief.

"We have a cabinet meeting tomorrow," said Lord Balfour. "I will discuss it more fully with Lord Montague then, and find out exactly what his objections are. Then I will discuss it with you again."

"I will be looking forward to hearing from you," said Weizmann in a low voice, still overwhelmed by the new information.

At the cabinet meeting, Lord Balfour arose and stated his position to the group. "I am in favor of making a declaration granting Palestine to the Jews as a national homeland."

Then the trouble began. Lord Montague arose from his seat, pushed his sleeves up slightly, and launched his attack.

"The Jews in England," he announced, in deep, determined tones, "are a loyal constituent of His Majesty's government. We are not members of any other national or nationalistic group. We are not interested in leaving England, and we are not interested in creating a sovereign Jewish State for Jews to reside in. We are happly to live here as British subjects who follow the religion of Moses."

Lord Balfour, a non-Jew, took his turn to speak, and challenged Lord Montague. "That may be true for some Jewish people in England. But Jews in other countries are not as secure as you are here, and have been driven from country to country for two thousand years! They have been wandering around the world ever since their eviction from their own homeland, Palestine, in the year 70, by the Romans!"

Montague rose again, this time in fury. He pounded his fists on the table and declared: "There is no Jewish *People!* Jews are members of the Mosaic faith. They have no national loyalties. Are you calling me an unfaithful citizen of England?"

"I am making no such charge, Lord Montague," replied Balfour, equally aroused. "I am not disputing your loyalty to Great Britain or that of any Jew in England. The fact is that there are many Jews in this country and elsewhere who would like to have a national homeland, whether they live there or not!" Then, turning to the other members of the cabinet, Balfour declared: "Who are we to believe? Lord Montague, or the rabbi from Jaffa? I am certain that the good rabbi knows better the desires of his people than Montague!"

Another member of the cabinet arose and put a temporary halt to the argument. "Let us take some time to investigate the matter. We cannot make a rash decision right now. Let us turn to the Jewish community and consult with their leaders, and see whether or not they truly want this national homeland."

Very soon after this cabinet meeting, word reached the Jewish community, through Dr. Weizmann, of what had happened. When Rabbi Kook received the news he was deeply disappointed. He was determined to see that the true opinion of the people reach the British authorities. He therefore drew up a letter to be circulated throughout England. He called it "A Manifesto Concerning the Act of National Treachery." The letter was read in every synagogue in England the following Sabbath morning. This is what it said:

"We protest publicly against those who would tear the Jewish soul apart; against those who wish to shatter the wonderful wholeness of Jews and Judaism. We only know a *whole* Judaism.

"This dispute, as to whether our national or religious assets constitute the content of our lives, is a bitter mockery. We demand full restitution for that which has been robbed from us. The crime which cries unto heaven must be completely corrected. Our precious, holy land, full of wonder and splendor; our pride, human rights and human dignity; our national and individual rights in all countries, must be returned to us completely, without compromises, without hypocrisy, entirely. . . .

"We are duty bound to explain to embattled humanity its obligations toward us. We gave much to humanity. In the ethics of mankind, we have inspired the power of life; our spiritual heritage pulsates in the inward substance of all cultured religions. . . .

"And the people have paid us back very 'beautifully' by robbing us of our land, exiling us from it and burning our Holy Temple; with massacres, with pogroms, with the fires of the auto de fa, with yellow badges. . . .

"And now, as we stand already at the end of the war. . . . is it not our duty in this awesome, wonderful and holy hour to inform all humanity, expecially the fighting cultured nations, that the crime of crimes will remain hanging over their heads if they will not cleanse themselves from the robbery and butchery that they have perpetrated against us? And that they will only make themselves even more miserable than the misery that they will inflict upon us? . . . .

"But, if, on the contrary, the results of the war will also bring about . . . our return and rehabilitation; if the nations will atone for the horrible crime and help us to organize ourselves fully on our land and to establish our own government, making it possible for us to rejuvenate and make fruitful our ancient ways of life – our calm, original, secular and holy, material and spiritual, brave and peaceful ways of life – then, the mark of eternal shame will be removed from the society of mankind. . . ."

Since most leaders of the Jewish people insisted strongly on achieving an independent Jewish state, Lord Balfour was able to swing the government to his view.

Finally, on November 2, 1917, Lord Balfour summoned Dr. Weizmann, Rabbi Kook, Lord Rothschild, and other Jewish dignitaries, to his office.

"I have very good news for you, gentlemen. A compromise has been worked out. The new version of the declaration for granting Palestine as a homeland to the Jews is slightly watered down, but we can still proclaim it. Your side has won the battle."

Tears came into the eyes of Rabbi Kook as he heard this good news. "This is a great moment in our lives," he said.

"One we will never forget," echoed Dr. Weizmann.

"Well, then, here is the document," said Lord Balfour. He then turned to Lord Rothschild.

"The letter is addressed to you, Lord Rothschild, as President of the British Zionist Federation. Let me read it to you:

> I have much pleasure in conveying to you, on behalf of His Majesty's Government, the following declaration of sympathy with Jewish Zionist aspirations which has been submitted to, and approved by, the Cabinet. His Majesty's Government, views with favour the establishment in Palestine of a national home for the Jewish people, and will use their best endeavours to facilitate the achievement of this object, it being clearly understood that nothing shall be done which may prejudice the civil and religious rights and political status enjoyed by Jews in any other country. I should be grateful to you if you would bring this declaration to the knowledge of the Zionist Federation."

The way was finally paved for the creation of the State of Israel.

Rabbi Kook did not view the granting of the "Balfour Declaration," (as it has been known since) as a *favor* to the Jewish people, but as a *duty* which the British government was obligated to perform.

A great celebration took place a short time after the declaration was pronounced, in Albert Hall in London. All of London's Jews were present to cheer the new declaration as the greatest event in Jewish history in two thousand years.

On the speaker's platform were Dr. Chaim Weizmann, Lord Rothschild, Rabbi Kook, and others. After Weizmann had finished his speech, Rabbi Kook rose to speak:

"I did not come to thank the English people," he said, "for the declaration that it gave us; I came rather to congratulate it, with the blessing of *mazal tov* on its great merit in being the one nation to grant us this declaration. The purpose of the existence of the whole world is the Torah, and he who attaches himself to the Torah is joined unto the eternity of God . . . It is the unique pride and glory of your nation, then, to lend aid and support to the people of the Torah. . . . On this do I congratulate the people of England – on their being counted among the supporters of the people of the Torah."

Thirty years later, in the same month, November, a vote was taken in the newly formed United Nations, and the majority cast their ballot for the creation of a Jewish state in Palestine, confirming the Balfour Declaration. This was in November, 1947. Six months later, in May, 1948, the State of Israel came into being.

Rabbi Kook's presence in London during this important historical crisis proved, therefore, to be of great significance.

As significant as it was, though, the existence of the Balfour Declaration did not leave the Jewish community without its battles. A forceful objection was made to the contents of the declaration, again by a group of Jews. Rabbi Kook immediately braced himself for this next ideological struggle.

15

"FLAG OF JERUSALEM"

Immediately after the promulgation of the Balfour Declaration, the leaders of the ultra-orthodox *Agudat Yisrael* called a meeting of its followers to protest the action.

At the meeting, the chairman rose to express his view of the recent turn of events.

"Gentlemen," he began, "a very serious mistake has been perpetrated upon us by two forces working together – the irreligious, secular Zionists, and the *Mizrachi,* whose viewpoint was presented by Rabbi Kook of Jaffa, now in London. We oppose the action taken because we want only religious Jews to return to the Holy Land. God gave us this land to further the causes of the holy Torah, not to be a political refuge for those who are not God-fearing."

Unknown to the *Agudah* members, a *Mizrachi* adherent was sitting in the last row of the meeting hall. Suddenly he jumped from his seat and shouted forth his answer to the remarks of the speaker.

"Can you deny a place in the Holy Land to a Jew as great as Chaim Weizmann?"

The chairman was at first surprised to hear someone interrupt his speaking, but decided to answer him.

"Dr. Weizmann may be a great scientist. But as long as he does not obey God's Torah he is not, in my mind, to be considered a good Jew."

The *Mizrachi* "spy" came back with: "How can one deny the love of Chaim Weizmann for the Jewish people and the Jewish Nation?"

"I am not denying his love for our people," answered the chairman, "but that is not enough. I would prefer that he be loyal to God rather than to the Jewish people."

"Being loyal to the Jewish people is part of being loyal to God!" shouted the Mizrachi member. "At least in the beginning! Loyalty to God can come out of following His ways as a nation." He then sat down, having finished what he had to say.

Then the chairman urged the *Agudah* to draft a letter to the British government in which the members would explain their position.

"We want our Jewish State to be proclaimed," they wrote, "by the Messiah sent by God, not by Lord Balfour or the British Cabinet. And that time will come when all Jews are deserving of redemption, by virtue of their adherence to the Law of God, the Torah."

Jews around the world were shocked at this opposition. At a time when thousands of Jews were seeking a place to live without being harassed by hostile nations, this was no action to take. When Jews had come closer than they had ever been in two thousand years to regaining their independence, this group committed what most Jews thought to be treason by siding with the enemy and placing a stumbling block in the path of their own people.

Rabbi Kook was on most occasions a very congenial person, resisting the temptation to take sides in a conflict, and attempting always to reconcile opposing forces. In this instance, however, he could not hold back. In a letter to an orthodox historian, the well known Zev Yavitz, he charged the *Agudah* with harboring unjustified negative feeling towards Zionists.

"All interest in Jewish nationalism," wrote Rabbi Kook, "is alien to them. They conceive of the Jewish people in a narrow-minded and one-sided way. Their vision of Judaism is a shrunken image."

"Perhaps they are content," he continued, "to bury their faces in the ground like ostriches. But I think that the Jewish people has more pride and dignity and bearing than that. Why should we live at the mercy of other nations and pick crumbs from their tables? Where is our self-respect and pride?"

TIME FOR A NEW ORGANIZATION?

It was at this time, in 1918, just at the end of World War I, that Rabbi Kook thought the time was ripe. for a new organization in Jewish life, one that would foster religious Zionism.

The *Agudah,* as a religious as it was, was certainly not the answer to modern Jews who wished to combine their religious devotion to Judaism with national loyalty to the Jewish people.

On the other hand, the *Mizrachi* group was officially part of the Zionist Organization itself. Included in the Zionist statement of principles was the sentence that "Zionism has nothing to do with religion." Many religious Jews, therefore, refused to become part of the *Mizrachi.*

Rabbi Kook saw the need for a third group, one which would avoid the extremes of the other two. It would be Zionist, as the *Agudah* was not, but it would be totally religious, as the parent body of the *Mizrachi* was not.

"This group," he thought, "would further the cause of Jewish religion in the Holy Land." He called it *Degel*

Yerushalayim (Flag of Jerusalem).

In the beginning, many rabbis tried to discourage him. "Why make yet another organization?" they asked. "There are two already. Besides, how can one man single-handedly organize a large international movement?"

"It will not be a simple task," agreed Rabbi Kook. "But after a short while I am sure that I will find many sympathetic followers. Then I will have many lieutenants to carry forward the program."

Rabbi Kook held mass meetings, wrote scores of letters, delivered speeches, and did everything he could to try to stimulate the growth of this new movement.

At one of the founding meetings, he explained the purpose of the new group as follows:

"My purpose is to establish many groups under the name *Degel Yerushalayim*, that shall indeed stand in a fraternal relation to general Zionism, but not as a branch of its formal organization. All these societies should be united for the goal of reviving the nation and the land on God's holy foundation, to establish the new life of those who return to His chosen land on the basis of illuminating the soul in its pure and natural source, to establish great schools of learning, a supreme rabbinical court, to stimulate literary work . . . "

Chapters were formed in every country that had heard of Rabbi Kook. But because there were already in existence two strong orthodox Jewish groups, the *Agudah* and the *Mizrachi*, this third movement found no room to breathe. It was, one might say, smothered to death between the other two. In addition, Rabbi Kook did not have the experience necessary to administer a vast organization. He was more the pious scholar than the community organizer.

He soon realized how foolish he had been to venture into such a vast project. His friends had been right after all: there was no room for a new organization. In a letter to a leader of one of the local chapters of *Degel Yerushalaym* Rabbi Kook explained the demise of the idea in the following words:

"I am not a politician and I cannot concern myself with matters which lead to divisiveness of thought. I see only the good side of every phenomenon, and to it I place myself in an attitude of appreciation and love. Therefore, I hope that even from the movement of *Agudat Yisrael* some good will come for the House of Israel. . . . We say 'shalom' to all, and we reveal that the light of holiness dwells also in secular Zionism which is founded upon the Love of Israel in its land. . . . We need the mercy of heaven in order that we might not be caught in the trap of narrowness of heart which leads to fault-finding and quarrel-seeking."

In short, Rabbi Kook was admitting that he did not possess the competitive spirit necessary for founding and furthering a mass movement. And so his idea died, as did the projects of his two rabbinical magazines. His idealism shielded him from reality, and he could not protect himself from the harshness of modern organizational and political life.

When the First World War ended and the nations began to put the pieces together and heal their political, social, economic, and spiritual wounds, Palestine, too, had a more settled life for a while. The Jewish territories were now under British rule, and an organized political and religious life was beginning to take form.

Since travel was now again possible, Rabbi Kook set his eyes once again to Jerusalem, his mission in England more or less completed.

In the year 1919 he received an invitation to become Chief Rabbi of the holy city of Jerusalem.

He informed the leaders of *Machzikey Ha-Dat* that what he had warned them about originally had come true. The opportunity to return to the Holy Land took precedence over the many pleasant friendships and associations he had developed in London.

He said his good-byes, packed his belongings, and returned home once again. This time he was never to leave Palestine again.

16

CHIEF RABBI KOOK

Since there was no institution yet of a "Chief Rabbinate" for all Eretz Yisrael, Rabbi Kook now held the highest position in Palestine, Chief Rabbi of the holy city of Jerusalem.

For many reasons, his position was now much more important than the one he had held in Jaffa five years before. Even though his influence went beyond the boundaries of his own congregation, the community in Jaffa was much smaller than the one in Jerusalem. And since Jerusalem was the *holy city,* there was more prestige and power attached to its rabbis, particularly its senior rabbi.

It did not take Rabbi Kook long to survey the religious situation in Palestine in 1919 and to compile a list of the major problems. The greatest difficulty he found as a leader of the Jewish people was the large number of differing factions of the people.

At a meeting of all of the rabbis of Jerusalem, Rabbi Kook expressed his hopes for a unification of all the differing groups:

"In the Diaspora, we Jews have always had strong differences among the many sections of the population. But in Eretz Yisrael there is no room for division and lack of agreement. We must work shoulder to shoulder to rebuild Palestine and create a national home for our people."

ENTER SIR HERBERT SAMUEL

The real impetus for organizing the rabbinate of the Holy Land under one central office came from an outside source.

Rabbi Kook received a letter one morning from Sir Herbert Samuel, a British Jew, representing the King of England. He said in the letter that he wanted to meet with Rabbi Kook and other leading rabbis about an important issue.

"What could Sir Herbert want?" Rabbi Kook asked one of the rabbis who had been in Palestine for several years.

"Whatever it is," replied the rabbi, "it must be important. Sir Herbert is a very powerful figure in Palestine."

"What do you mean?" asked Rabbi Kook.

"I'll have to explain what happened in Palestine during your absence for you to completely understand."

"Please do," answered Rabbi Kook. "I would like to know exactly what Sir Herbert's status here is.."

"Of course, you remember when General Allenby's British Forces took Palestine from the Turks last year. After that, the English placed in Palestine a High Commissioner, responsible to the British Colonial Office in London. This man is Sir Herbert Samuel. Since Britain actually has full political charge over the country, his authority has great importance. Sir Herbert represents the King himself."

Thus, Rabbi Kook answered Sir Herbert's letter and arranged a meeting.

The day for the meeting arrived, and Sir Herbert entered the office of the Chief Rabbi of Jerusalem.

"Rabbi Kook," he said, "I have a problem which I think

you could help solve."

"I will be most happy and honored to help such a distinguished person as you in any way I can, naturally," replied the rabbi in a friendly manner.

"My government," began Sir Herbert, "is extremely interested in having the population in Palestine rule themselves as much as possible. We are here to help and supervise, but we want the peoples living here to make their own rules and enforce them. This is particularly important in religious areas."

"I agree," said Rabbi Kook, happily. "I think this is an excellent policy, and I am glad your government feels that way."

"With regard to religious matters," continued the High Commissioner, "we want the Christians living here to handle their marriage, divorce, and other religious matters according to the tenets of their faith. The same for the Mohammedans. And, of course, the Jews also. I think, Rabbi Kook, that it would be to the best interest of the Jewish community in Palestine if there were one rabbi who had total charge over all religious matters for Jews. This will also simplify my job of supervision over the country. I can then have one man to turn to, who can tell me what the problems are and how they can be solved."

"That would indeed make matters very simple and efficient," said Rabbi Kook with a reflective smile on his face. The idea sounded excellent to him. "In this way we can establish a central religious office for the country, with a central assembly of rabbis to make laws and decide difficult religious questions – all under the authority of the Chief Rabbi of Palestine."

"The question I have to ask you since you know your people better than I do, is how to go about organizing such a central office and selecting the man to lead it."

"The only way to do that," replied the Chief Rabbi of

Jerusalem, "is to convene an assembly of rabbis and laymen from all over Palestine and *vote* for the Chief Rabbi."

Plans were made and much thought was given to the new institution of the Chief Rabbinate. After months of planning, the meeting suggested by Rabbi Kook was finally called.

At the meeting many people expressed their opinions. One tall, bearded man with a dark complexion arose and began to address those present.

"I think it wise to have a Chief Rabbi," he said, "but will he be *Ashkenazic* or *Sephardic?"*

Living in Palestine were European Jews, who were called *Ashkenazim,* from countries like Russia, Poland, Germany, England, and Eastern Jews, called *Sephardim,* from North Africa, Syria, Iraq, etc. Both of them had their own sets of laws and rituals which, though basically the same, had many variations which made them separate and distinct.

"How can an *Ashkenazic* Rabbi decide questions of Law for the *Sephardic* Jews, and vice versa?" the man continued.

A second speaker rose. He was a medium-size strong-looking man, with rimless glasses. "I have an idea," he said. "Why can't we have two Chief Rabbis, one for the *Ashkenazim* and one for the *Sephardim?"*

This suggestion seemed acceptable to everyone, and so *two* rabbis were to be elected. This system of two Chief Rabbis exists to this day.

One of the delegates came up to the rostrum and spoke to the audience about his choice for the first Chief Rabbi of Palestine.

"Only one rabbi exists, my dear friends, in all Eretz Yisrael, and in all the world, who is universally accepted as leader of all Jews. He is the only one who can rally to himself all of the forces working for the good of our people. He is a scholar, a pious and humble person, and an outstanding rabbi. All of us humbly ask Rabbi Abraham Isaac Hakohen Kook to become our first Chief Rabbi!"

The people in attendance rose to their feet, and offered an overwhelming applause to confirm the opinion of the speaker.

In great joy, Rabbi Kook, Chief Rabbi of Jerusalem, accepted the title of Chief Rabbi of Palestine. He rose to make a short speech:

"If the people sincerely feel that I am the one they want as Chief Rabbi, then I can hardly refuse doing this great service to God and His people. I shall try to do as good a job as possible. I will serve my people because I love each and every one of them. All the Jewish people are equally dear to me, whatever their position in life or whatever their religious philosophy. I love all creation and all people, but especially the Jewish people."

And so, in 1921, at age fifty-six, Rabbi Abraham Isaac Kook became the religious leader of all of Palestine.

For *Sephardic* Chief Rabbi, the group voted for Rabbi Meir Frank, also a pious and learned man.

Despite the overwhelming approval that Rabbi Kook received from rabbis and laymen all over the Holy Land, as their new Chief Rabbi, there was one small element of the population which refused to accept him. This led the new Chief Rabbi into another public conflict, one which aroused bitter emotions throughout Palestine.

17

RABBI AGAINST RABBI

There was one leading rabbi in Jerusalem who, together with some of his followers, refused to accept the new Chief Rabbi. His name was Rabbi Joseph Chaim Sonnenfeld.

Every time he had to refer to Rabbi Kook, he called him "the Rabbi of Jaffa," rather than recognize his new title, "Chief Rabbi." Every decision made by the new Chief Rabbi was opposed by Rabbi Sonnenfeld.

What reason could this rabbi have for acting in such a way? Was it personal rivalry? Jealousy? It was none of these base motives. In fact, it was a very noble motive, even though a mistaken one. Rabbi Sonnenfeld was a very pious person, but was led astray by his extreme zealousness. Sometimes too much of a good thing can become a bad thing. This was apparently the case with Rabbi Sonnenfeld.

What troubled Rabbi Sonnenfeld was that Rabbi Kook was cooperating with the non-religious Jews and sympathized with them.

In his zeal for strict observance of the old way of life, Rabbi Sonnenfeld saw danger in anything that was new or different from the way in which he lived and practiced his religion.

To Rabbi Sonnenfeld, the Jews, as God's chosen people, were so special and unique that it was incumbent upon them to resist copying any custom or pattern of life practiced by non-Jews.

The Jew, he believed, should be educated only by God's Torah, and pursuit of secular knowledge and foreign languages was therefore considered a grave evil.

Several years before Rabbi Kook arrived in Palestine, Rabbi Sonnenfeld actually pronounced a ban of excommunication upon anyone who studied languages other than Hebrew. This meant that all Jews who followed Rabbi Sonnenfeld as their religious leader could not go within four paces of such a person, nor could they communicate with him in any way.

After the ban was pronounced, a certain man in Jerusalem, Mr. Joshua Yellin, decided that his son David, a very bright young man, should attend a school which taught foreign languages. (David Yellin, by the way, later became a great scholar in Hebrew and other Semitic languages.)

When Rabbi Sonnenfeld found out about this, he went to the synagogue and declared, before a large crowd:

"Joshua Yellin has sent his son to a cursed school. He is thus excommunicated, and we are not to recognize him any more or speak to him. He will no longer receive funds from the central agency of the Jewish community."

This was a serious move. Owing to poor farming conditions and small profits from business, most people depended on these funds for their living. Those distributing the funds were under the control of Rabbi Sonnenfeld, who thus had a great deal of power in the community.

Yellin was determined not to be bullied by what he called a "narrow-minded rabbi." He sent his son David to the school in defiance of the threat.

"I don't care if he throws a million bans upon me," exclaimed Mr. Yellin in flushed anger. "He cannot chain my mind nor the mind of my young son. We will use our brains for the purpose God gave them to us, to study whatever intellectual pursuits are open to us."

Rabbi Sonnenfeld fulfilled his pronouncement. He cut off funds from the Yellin family and had all of his followers dissociate themselves from him.

Although all of Rabbi Sonnenfeld's followes accepted his decree, many more open-minded rabbis did not. Indeed there were many orthodox Jews who were supporters of a more lenient and enlightened attitude towards "outside" learning. These people withheld their support from the ban.

Nevertheless, Mr. Yellin had a difficult time finding money for his family to live and go to school. He pleaded with rabbis all over Palestine, and all over Europe through the mails, but the ban was a mighty weapon and had disastrous effects. The Yellin Family had to live on the smallest budget possible.

All of the foregoing transpired before Rabbi Kook came to Palestine so that he had no control over it. Even after his arrival, Rabbi Sonnenfeld continued his narrow-minded opposition to secular learning.

"I will have no contact with free-thinking atheists," said Rabbi Sonnenfeld to Rabbi Kook after the latter's election to the post of Chief Rabbi of Jerusalem. "If you wish to cooperate with such as they, then I will oppose your office and everything you do. You are being fooled by these sinners, and will eventually bring a curse upon yourself and the entire household of Israel."

When the Jews of Jerusalem organized themselves into a "Community Council for Jerusalem Jews," Rabbi Sonnenfeld's followers formed their own council of "*Ashkenazic* Jews in Jerusalem." Any group or organization in which anyone but strictly observant Jews participated was banned by this zealous sage.

When the time came to form a Chief Rabbinate for the entire *Yishuv* (Palestinian Jewry), an assembly was convened of members from all walks of life. Rabbi Sonnenfeld then expressed his objection to such a Chief Rabbinate being chosen by *all* Jews, religious and non-religious.

"The Chief Rabbi of Palestine," he declared in fierce anger, "must be selected by a small group of strictly traditional rabbis. No layman, especially no non-observant Jew, can have any say in such a weighty matter."

Others felt that to win wide support for the new office of Chief Rabbinate, it would be necessary to have the broadest possible base of electors. The whole community would have to express their views in order for them ultimately to accept his authority. This was a logical and democratic, as well as diplomatic move. But not for Rabbi Sonnenfeld who maintained that God's Law did not bend for anyone. To him, God's Law was clear. There was only one way to do things: the old way.

The situation reached the point at which Rabbi Sonnenfeld declared anything new automatically evil.

For example, the High Commissioner of Palestine arranged with Chief Rabbi Kook to create an Appelate Religious Court (court of appeals) and a Supreme Religious Court, as in the legal systems of other countries. Rabbi Sonnenfeld looked in the Torah, and, not finding any such thing there, declared it null and void.

"If the other nations have one, then we are copying them," he declared. "And to copy other nations is forbidden by the Torah. We have our own wonderful system of law, and it needs no improvement."

When the day finally came for the first Chief Rabbi of Palestine to be elected, Rabbi Sonnenfeld declared it a day of fasting and mourning. His followers wore sackcloth and sprinkled ashes on themselves as a sign of their grief. They touched no food or water that entire day.

"The Chief Rabbinate," said the rabbi, "is the product of cooperation with the spiritual enemy – the ignorant and impious Jews in our community. We must oppose them and lend them no support."

Later, when the Community Council of Jerusalem approached its members for contributions to the support of the community, Rabbi Sonnenfeld and his followers refused to pay. When elections were held, they refused to vote.

They created their own synagogues, schools, charities, courts, and council. There was to be no contact with the "heretics."

Despite all of the disagreements Rabbi Kook had with this formidable opponent – and with others like him – he remained cheerful and undaunted. When friends tried to hinder differences of opinion, Rabbi Kook stopped them.

"I don't need anyone to shield me," he said. "If I had no one to disagree with, I would have to hire people to oppose me."

Thus, in all of his dealings with his ideological opponents, Rabbi Kook showed himself to be a "perfect saint."

18

THE PERFECT SAINT

If it is possible to pin-point one specific attitude which molded the actions of Rabbi Kook, it was his love for the people of Israel – for all Jews everywhere.

Being a man of deep religious convictions and living in a generation which rebelled violently against everything he taught and stood for, he could have let himself fall prey to despondency and frustration. He had many good reasons to be discouraged and give up. While he preached observance of religious obligations and study of holy books, most of the pioneer youth settling the Land paid more attention to the study of books by Marx, Engels, and other socialists. But this did not cause Rabbi Kook to feel hopeless frustration. His depth of understanding and his sympathetic attitude towards the problems of the new age helped him retain hope for their ultimate return to authentic Judaism.

His fellow rabbis often chided him: "How can you show so much sympathy for these young atheistic renegades? They are destroying Judaism!"

Rabbi Kook answered this charge with a parable. "The Land of our fathers is holy," he began. "The city of

Jerusalem is more holy than any other city in the Holy Land. The temple on Mount Zion was the most holy place in the Holy City. And the sacred room in the temple known as the Holy of Holies was the most holy place in the holy temple." The curiosity of his listeners increased as they began to wonder what this had to do with their question.

"Only the High Priest," Rabbi Kook continued, "could enter this Holy of Holies, and he could enter only on the most holy day of the year, Yom Kippur (the Day of Atonement). And even then, he could enter only after having gone through an elaborate ritual of purification. Yet, when the Holy of Holies needed repair, any simple workman could enter on any day, with no special ceremony, with his soiled working clothes and tools, to do his painting and hammering."

"The same is true," he pointed out, "of the land of Israel. Right now we are in the stage of repairing our Holy Land. While the building is taking place, all the detailed laws of holiness and religious observance are suspended until the Land is once again ready for divine service.

"These dedicated young people have come to rebuild our Land at great personal sacrifice. Their work is hard, their hours are long, and their reward is small. They are saintly people in their own way. Like all Jews, they have a divine spark within them that needs merely to be fanned to grow into a burning flame of love for God.

"The soul of the Jew is innately pious. Whenever it occurs that a Jew does not appear to be pious, this is only a superficial judgment, a temporary situation. With the passage of time, his real, noble self will emerge.

"Many of the lapses in our national religious life which exist today are due to the unusual hardships we've experienced during many years of exile. Being far from our homeland, we have slipped into complacency; being persecuted has warped our true nature. We did not have the advantage of breathing the holy and pure air of Eretz Yisrael.

But now, with the great redemption taking place, the therapeutic quality of the Land will revive us and cure our spiritual ills."

Once a visitor from Denver, Colorado, complained to the rabbi about the lack of religiosity he found during his visit to the Holy Land.

"Here I am in the Land of our Fathers," he said, "where I expected everyone to be deeply observant and pious, and I find the opposite."

Rabbi Kook pretended to ignore his remarks for a moment, and changed the subject.

"Tell me," he asked his visitor, "what kind of place is Denver? I have heard that it is filled with tubercular people. It must be a very unhealthy city."

The visitor became insulted and promptly replied, "On the contrary. It is precisely because of the wonderful healing quality of our climate that people who are sick come from all over the world to be healed."

"Don't you see," said the rabbi, "that this is precisely the situation with us in Palestine? Our great healing climate attracts people who are spiritually ill. In the holy atmosphere of Eretz Yisrael, they, too, will be healed."

On another occasion, a Jerusalem rabbi tried to persuade Rabbi Kook not to invite so many non-religious people to his home. "Why do you always throw your doors wide open to secular leaders and impious Zionists?"

"I have proof of the righteousness of my actions from God himself," answered the rabbi. "Do we not say in the Yom Kippur prayers, 'Thou, O Lord, givest Thy hand to sinners . . . ?'

"Furthermore, one of our Hasidic masters advises us that 'In order to love one who is not completely wicked, it is enough if we are not completely pious; but in order to love one who is completely wicked, it is necessary to be completely pious.' "

Rabbi Kook contended that merely *living* in Eretz Yisrael was a great *mitzvah,* and that those who came to settle in the Land of their Fathers were taking the first step towards a religious life. All of the Jewish people, he felt, were holy, but expecially those living in the Holy Land. Often he would sign his letter, "Rabbi Abraham Isaac Hakohen Kook, Servant of a Holy People in the Holy Land."

When his colleagues disagreed with his attitude, he would answer them by quoting the Talmudic injunction that "One must not pray in a room without windows." "This means," he explained, "that when we pray we must be able to see outside of ourselves, to look out through the windows of our hearts at the suffering and the longing of our brethren. It means that we must not pray in the narrow confines of our own feelings, but we must include in our prayers *all* Israel."

This did not satisfy the rabbis who continued viewing with dismay the phenomenon of an irreligious generation of young Jews. "Rabbi Kook," they reprimanded him, "your love for these young people may be false a love."

"Better a false love, dear colleagues," was his reply, "than a false hatred. What we need among our people is much more of such 'false love' – love with no ulterior motive."

Trying to hide his impatience, he replied: "You have no confidence in the strength of the Holy Land to affect its inhabitants with its religious spirit. Our country is being built now, like a house rising from the ground. When one looks at a house in the process of construction, it looks untidy, with all the materials and tools strewn about and the builders in soiled garments. It lacks order and form.

"But once the house is finished, the builders can clean the house and themselves. So shall it be with the observance of Judaism. When our house, Eretz Yisrael, is rebuilt – when the swamps are drained, the land irrigated, the mosquitoes expunged, the cities carved into shape – then we can clean ourselves of the building debris and use our time to cultivate our religious and cultural spirit. Right now, our national effort must take precedence, so that the pace of the construction and the rebuilding does not slacken."

Rabbi Kook was thrilled when the great Russian-born Hebrew poet, Chaim Nachman Bialik, came to settle in Palestine. Bialik was not a traditionally observant Jew, but his poems were deeply imbued with a sense of piety, respect for tradition, and love for his fellow Jews and their sacred history.

Some of the religious leaders in the *Yishuv* were disappointed at Bialik's arrival. "He's a *goy* (in the category of a gentile)," they proclaimed in scorn.

Rabbi Kook, in his capacity of Chief Rabbi, wrote Bialik a glowing letter of welcome. He knew that if the spirit of the Jewish people were to be resurrected, it would have to be revived with the replenishment of Hebraic culture: poetry, music, and art.

For the same reason, he was happy to see the foundation of the Bezalel School of Fine Arts, while others had reservations about it because of the possibility of violating the commandment: "Thou shalt not make unto thyself a graven image."

In the 1920's, a group of Jewish intellectual leaders decided that the time was ripe for founding a national university, where students from all parts of Palestine could study for degrees in higher learning. It was to be called "The Hebrew University," and the site chosen for its location was beautiful Mount Scopus.

When the buildings were completed, in 1925, Rabbi Kook received an invitation to attend the dedication ceremony and offer a prayer for the future growth and welfare of the new university.

Many rabbis strongly objected to the existence of such a university. "They will teach science and other secular studies," they argued, "which will cause further neglect of our ancient traditions. And even if there is a program for the study of the Bible and traditional holy works, they are likely to be taught by non-observant teachers, and attended by students without the traditional head-covering."

But Rabbi Kook viewed the university from a different perspective. He welcomed it, because he saw in the broadest realms of knowledge the gift of God. Learning to use the gifts of nature was fulfilling the commandment for man to be a partner with God in the ever-renewing creation of the world.

Rabbi Kook wasted no time in writing a letter of acceptance to the university, saying: "I welcome the dedication of these buildings of the Hebrew University as a significant event in Jewish life. This great institution will fulfill the need to centralize Jewish academic learning and to provide a place where the new generation can receive a broad and thorough education."

Soon thereafter, the Conservative Movement of Judaism in America planned to build a synagogue in Jerusalem. It was suspected among the Orthodox that this Movement, which attempted to modify some of the traditional practices of the Jewish religion, would weaken the texture of Jewish life in Palestine, and that the building of their own synagogue would contribute to the future growth of this Movement and plant seeds of "modernism" in the holy soil.

Nevertheless, the time soon came for laying the cornerstone of this synagogue, now known as the Yeshurun Synagogue in Jerusalem, and an invitation was sent to Rabbi Kook to participate in the ceremony.

"I welcome the building of this synagogue," he wrote back. "Anything which will foster the spirit of religion in Palestine is, in my eyes, a positive action."

Rabbi Kook's interest and support was not limited to the events in Jewish life which betokened modernization; he also saw the need for preserving the traditional, that which was venerated in antiquity and had been sanctified by history.

It happened once that a moden-thinking educator condemned one of the old *Yeshivot* as a school that neglected modern subjects and did not employ the latest pedagogic techniques.

"We cannot destroy the old or the new," Rabbi Kook admonished him. "Each has its important place in the scheme of things."

It was then that Rabbi Kook formulated his famous motto, which summarized his whole life's writings, speeches, teachings, actions, and thinking:

"Let the old be renewed, and the new become hallowed." In the original Hebrew, this phrase takes the form of a rime: Hayashan yitchadesh, ve-hechadash yitkadesh."

19

THE MURDER OF CHAIM ARLOSSOROFF

One hot Friday evening in Tel Aviv, June, 1933, a young, dynamic leader of the *Yishuv,* Chaim Arlossoroff, was walking along the dark shores of the Mediterranean ocean with his wife, Sima.

Arlossoroff took advantage of the Sabbath hours to spend some moments with his wife because his time-consuming position as head of the political department of the Jewish Agency, and leader of the Labor Union *(Histadrut),* did not leave him any time during the week for leisure.

It was a dark, moonless night, and the soft sound of the waves breaking on the shore soothed the tired leader. As they strolled along the coast, Sima Arlossoroff heard footsteps. She turned and saw two men. One came closer and asked Dr. Arlossoroff for the time. As he began to take out his watch, the other stranger pulled out a revolver and shot him. The two men then fled.

Sima screamed as she watched her husband fall limp onto the wet sand. But before anyone could get to them, the strangers had disappeared into the darkness. Dr. Arlossoroff was rushed to a nearby hospital and emergency surgery was performed, but to no avail. He was dead.

The next day the entire *Yishuv* was in an uproar. One of the most prominent young men of the country had been taken from them. Who would commit such a dastardly act?

Since the assassination took place on a moonless night and in an out-of-the-way spot, there was little hope of finding the murderers.

Yet, not too long after the murder was committed, a certain Abraham Stavsky was apprehended and charged with the crime.

Stavsky was a member of the Revisionists, a political group which was bitterly opposed to the *Histadrut*. These two groups, the *Histadrut* and the *Revisionists*, were enemies from their very inception since their basic philosophies were totally divergent. *Histadrut* was a moderate, peace-loving labor organization of Jewish workers, while the Revisionists were militant extremists who would resort to arms at the slightest provocation.

Since there had been so many bitter fights and ideological clashes between these two groups, members of the *Histadrut* immediately suspected that their leader had been killed by a Revisionist.

The finger was pointed at Abraham Stavsky, and eventually, enough evidence was mustered to bring him to trial. A great deal of bitterness accompanied the trial. The murder of the thirty-four year old Dr. Arlossoroff had merely added fuel to the already flaming-hot relations between the *Histadrut* and the Revisionists.

The members of the *Histadrut* were therefore emotionally involved in the trial, and, blinded by their bitter feelings, they declared Stavsky guilty even before the trial began.

They were out for revenge more than justice, and launched a country-wide campaign for Stavsky's conviction. Mass publicity was given to the trial throughout the settlements of the *Yishuv*, and it soon became the daily topic of conversation.

Finally, the day of the verdict arrived. The people in the courtroom sat spellbound as one of the three British judges who presided rose from his seat and read the verdict:

"Abraham Stavsky, you are found guilty by a majority of this court. Your sentence is death by hanging."

While members of the *Histadrut* were happy that their revenge was being fulfilled, the few impartial witnesses that were to be found felt that the evidence was insufficient and that the trial was a miscarriage of justice. The case was assigned to a Court of Appeals.

RABBI KOOK HEARS THE NEWS

When news of the conviction reached the home of Chief Rabbi Kook, he could not believe what he heard.

"How could they possibly convict this man when there is not a shred of solid evidence proving his guilt?" cried Rabbi Kook to his wife. "How can people turn a political struggle into a personal vendetta of this type? People are more interested in putting the Revisionists on trial than seeing the truth come to light."

Later that evening, Rabbi Kook sat in his kitchen in a very depressed mood. Some neighbors came to his house and joined him in a cup of tea.

"Why are you so depressed, Rabbi?" they asked.

"I am shocked at the news of the conviction that I heard today. It defeats the whole purpose of this redemption. Jews are returning to Eretz Yisrael to be purified from the contamination of living in exile. There, justice was often impossible for our people. Here, in the Holy Land, it *must* reign supreme. Where is the vision of justice and righteousness envisioned by the prophets and sages of our people?"

Immediately, Rabbi Kook plunged into a vigorous campaign to have the decision reversed. As the Sabbath hour approached, he hurriedly scribbled an urgent message to a group of friends who shared his feelings on the trial, and sent it by messenger with a request that it be printed on handbills for wide distribution among the public.

The message read as follows:

> Fellow Jews: Innocent blood will be shed unless we come to the aid of Abraham Stavsky. I can testify before God and man that he is innocent of all guilt. The decision of the judges was based on trumped-up charges. The one judge who cleared Stavsky is in the right. Anyone who has the spark of the divine within him will protest this sin and save an innocent soul from the gallows. Do not allow this perversion of justice to be carried through.

That evening, in his home, Rabbi Kook welcomed the Sabbath with sweet grape wine and wished the members of his household a peaceful Sabbath. But the peacefulness was soon interrupted by a visiting neighbor who told him that at that very moment, during the Holy Sabbath, people were pasting his message on the walls and signboards throughout the holy city of Jerusalem!

"This violation of the Sabbath," continued the guest, "will be exploited by your enemies. They will ridicule your attempts to have the Sabbath observed when you yourself desecrate it."

Rabbi Kook found himself in an embarassing position and, at first, did not know how to answer.

"I did not know they would begin displaying the notices so quickly. I just finished writing it a few hours ago. On the other hand, I did urge that the publicity be arranged as urgently and quickly as possible. But, on the holy Sabbath!? What shall we do now?"

He sat for a minute and thought, with his elbow resting on the table and his fist supporting his jaw.

"You know," he said, after reflecting for a while, "-

Jewish law demands that to save the life of one person, a million people are permitted to break a million Sabbaths. So, to save the life of this innocent man, certainly these few people can break one Sabbath."

Rabbi Kook continued to campaign during the following weeks for the exoneration of Abraham Stavsky. Many among the ranks of the *Histadrut* became enraged at him for protecting a "proven murderer." They were also resentful that he was trying to deprive them of their vengeance.

It took great courage to oppose the masses in this controversial trial. But to Rabbi Kook, what was right was more important than what was popular. A good leader, he reasoned, does not say what the people *want* to hear, but what they *should* hear. Thus, his leadership was very much in the tradition of Isaiah and Jeremiah and other great prophets.

In a letter to the newspaper of the *Mizrachi* Movement, he wrote as follows:

> From the bottom of my heart, which bleeds for the distress of my people, I wish to send this letter to you . . . . I testify before heaven and earth that my whole heart and soul are dedicated to the totality of our nation and to every one of its sections and parties, because I believe in perfect faith that every party is a particular limb in the sacred and wonderful organism of the whole congregation of Israel. . . .
>
> Only truth in its purity leads me to attempt to save him who was condemned to death with no grounds whatsoever for the accusation. I am completely permeated with the conviction that the accused is innocent and just and entirely pure of the slightest taint or suspicion of murder. And it is clear to me that no Jewish individual or group had anything to do with this murder.

The day of appeal arrived. People all over Palestine waited nervously for the verdict. Rabbi Kook prayed intensely each day of the new trial, and ordered that a prayer vigil be held around-the-clock in his Yeshiva.

At the end of the trial, a messenger knocked on the door of Rabbi Kook's home. "The crowds are shouting outside your door, Rabbi. They are shouting, 'Long live Rabbi Kook!' All three judges agreed in acquitting Stavsky from the crime."

"Thank the Lord," said Rabbi Kook, "for helping to remove this disgrace from our people. This decision is indeed a sanctification of God's name."

Stavsky himself came to Rabbi Kook's home and threw his arms around him in gratitude.

"Blessed be He who looseth the bound," said Rabbi Kook, pronouncing the ancient Hebrew blessing.

The people standing nearby answered "AMEN!"

That night Rabbi Kook slept well. He had struggled valiantly for justice and had won. But his rest was short-lived. Not long after the Stavsky affair a new and more threatening menace appeared to arouse him once again to tireless work for the welfare of the Jewish people.

20

THE WAILING WALL DISPUTE

Ever since a small stream of Jews began to settle in Palestine in the late nineteenth century, the Arab population was apprehensive about its new neighbors, as people usually are about strangers. They looked upon the Jews as enemies from another land, perhaps because they were afraid that the "outsiders" would change their way of life. Whatever the cause of such a fear, the Arab leaders exploited it by stirring their people against the Jewish "Invaders" at every opportunity. An outside "enemy," they reasoned, would help preserve the inner unity of the Arab peoples.

The most bitter enemy of the Zionist leaders was the Mufti (president) of the Supreme Moslem Council, Haj Amin el Husseini. He vowed to drive out the Jews and took every opportunity to incite conflicts.

One hot summer day in 1929, thousands of Jews came on a special pilgrimage from all over Palestine to the Wailing Wall. This wall is the eastern wall of the ancient temple, the only part of the temple still standing, and has been a Jewish shrine for centuries.

The day was a Jewish fast day known as *Tisha B'Av* (the

ninth day of the Hebrew month of *Av),* the anniversary of the destruction of the second Temple by the Romans in 70 C.E. (The first Temple was also destroyed on this day, in 586 B.C.E., by the Babylonians.) Tisha B'Av is therefore a day of religious mourning for Jews.

Arabs in the vicinity of the Wailing Wall began to get suspicious when the crowds formed. Some of the Arab leaders knew very well that this was a religious holiday but took advantage of the opportunity to fan the flames of bitterness between Arab and Jew.

"Look!" shouted one of the leaders to a throng of Arab onlookers, "the Jews are gathering to plan an attack on Arab shrines! Let us kill them before they attack!"

Immediately, a riot ensued and much blood was shed.

After the bloody riots, the Arabs insisted on claiming the sector in which the Wailing Wall was located as their territory. They insisted that Jews be forbidden to approach it.

RABBI KOOK CALLS A MEETING

Rabbi Kook objected violently to relinquishing this sacred shrine and quickly called a meeting of leading rabbis to plan their strategy in opposing the Arab claim.

"I think we should give up the wall," said one of the rabbis. "It is not worth causing bloodshed. Someday, soon, we shall retrieve it forever."

"How can you think so naively?" asked Rabbi Kook in surprise. "First of all, this is all that remains of our Holy Temple, the only remnant of our ancient glorious days of independence. These Arabs will gobble up more and more of our land and deny us more and more of our rights if we give in. We must not show them any sign of weakness. We must oppose them with all our strength. Otherwise, they will steal our land, desecrate our shrines and destroy our holy places."

Since the people at the meeting were divided in their opinion, Rabbi Kook decided to plead with the Jewish population and wrote a letter to the public, published in the Palestine newspapers.

This is what he wrote:

> There is a nation in the world, and Israel is its name. And of hoary age is this nation. Mighty forces have risen from time time, bent upon its extermination. Many and poweful forces assaulted its land, destroyed its sanctuary, scattered its sons to every corner of the world, and pursued them with zealous wrath. And this nation has a magnificent soul, ineradicable and of diverse potentialities, drawing its sustenance from the living power of the Creator.
>
> This people had a temple, more charged with holiness and sacred associations than any other sanctuary in the whole world. And when this land was devastated and the proud temple was razed to the ground, there was left for it only one remnant in the land of the living – that is our wall – the Wailing Wall. . .

When the Arabs saw that the Jews would not give up the wall peacefully, they made one massive attack on the *Yishuv*.

They plundered, murdered, and destroyed every Jewish settlement they could find in what was the bloodiest riot that Palestine had seen since the First World War. Jews were slaughtered in cold blood on their farms, in their homes, in villages and in study halls. It was merciless butchery. Five hundred Jews were put to death, and hundreds more wounded and maimed.

But with Rabbi Kook as their spiritual leader, the people maintained their hope and confidence. They tried to rebuild what property had been destroyed and continued their efforts towards making Palestine livable.

Since the end of World War One, the British were

charged with governing Palestine. Thus, the British government sent a commission to investigate the riots.

Lord Passfield, Colonial Secretary of Great Britain, a vigorous anti-Zionist, sent two investigating commissions. After three months, a report was published, expressing a totally one-sided point of view. To the utter shock and dismay of the Jewish community, the report (known as the Passfield White Paper) completely absolved the Mufti and his gangs of any guilt in the bloody massacres.

The commission declared that it was the fault of the increasing number of Jewish immingrants "flooding" Palestine. This influx, it claimed, was threatening the security of the Arabs. From then on, no further immigration of Jews would be permitted and no more land purchases were to be made by Jews.

This White Paper was an overt repudiation of the Balfour Declaration of 1917. The British were turning their backs on their previous commitment to placate the Arab majority. So vigorous was the outburst by world Jewry that the harsh measures were slightly softened shortly thereafter.

Through all of this deadly strife and bloody battling, Rabbi Kook pointed out to his people that the values of the spirit can never be taken away. It was this great recognition, he told them, which preserved the Jewish people through centuries of persecution. It would preserve them now as well. If they would only keep faith with their Maker and continue to work and build, God would not disappoint them. This was the Chief Rabbi's message.

Through these dark and hopeless days, the one ray of light and hope for the Jews was the soothing sermons and speeches of their beloved Chief Rabbi, whose shining model of patience, piety, and devotion to religious and humanitarian values, raised them from the depths of despair to the high peaks of creativity, once again.

But Rabbi Kook's days were getting shorter and his

strength was ebbing. His steadfast inspiration would not last forever, but while it did, there was no reason to fear. The pious and beloved saint was still in the midst of his people to give them hope, faith, and courage in the hour of their greatest testing.

21

SCHOLAR, EDUCATOR, AND MYSTIC

Rabbi Kook's personality was multifaceted.

First of all, he was a great scholar. From the earliest days in the *Yeshiva* when he was discovered to be an *Illui* (child prodigy), he spent the major portion of each day reading and studying.

Despite his heavy burden of activities in public life, he always managed to find time to study and to teach. Studying and teaching were his first great loves. His most thrilling moments were when he was surrounded by students and books.

Rabbis from all over the world wrote to him, asking for both personal advice and for decisions on complicated legal questions. His answers to these letters were recently published in Israel in four volumes.

He also wrote many other books, only a small number of which have been published so far. These works deal with Jewish law, philosophy, and religious thought. His commentary on the *Siddur* (prayerbook) is a favorite among Hebrew-reading Jews around the world. A publishing firm in Jerusalem, "The Rabbi Kook Foundation," is now publishing a collection of his works which will probably number well over thirty volumes before the series is complete.

Rabbi Kook's books show him to be a man of deep and broad leaning. He not only knew his own literary heritage, but that of other nations and cultures as well. His knowledge of other philosophies helped him see the Jewish religion in the larger context of world civilization.

Once, when the great scientist Albert Einstein came to Palestine, he paid a visit to the Chief Rabbi.

"I am honored indeed," said Einstein, "to be in the presence of one of our people's great spiritual gaints."

"It is I who am honored, revered Professor," answered Rabbi Kook. "A man of your stature in the scientific world appears only once in a century."

The discussion between the two men lasted an hour. Einstein had several other appointments to meet that day, and an aide had to remind him of the lateness of the hour.

"Never mind," said Einstein, "my discussion with Rabbi Kook is too interesting to interrupt. The others will have to wait. Rabbi Kook is one of the few people in the world who understand my 'Theory of Relativity.' "

RABBI KOOK THE TEACHER AND EDUCATOR

In addition to being a great scholar, he was a master educator and builder of schools. In cooperation withseveral organizations, he helped found dozens of Jewish elementary and high schools all over Palestine. Religious schools, trade schools, whatever the demand required, were all aided by Rabbi Kook.

To help create a large fund for the support of these institutions, Rabbi Kook led a delegation of rabbis from all over the world to the United States to raise the money.

The Chief Rabbi's most lasting achievement in education was the creation of his own *Yeshiva* in

Jerusalem, known as *Merkaz Ha-Rav,*Rabbi Kook's Central Academy. There he lectured to the many students who flocked around him all his days in the Holy land. He fought to make this institution one which would utilize modern as well as traditional approaches to jewish learning, in line with his general philosophy of achieving a harmonious blend between the old and the new.

His vision of a literary rebirth never ebbed, and in spite of his own unsuccessful attempts at founding journals, he encouraged his students to become creative contributors to the living literature of the Jewish people.

THE SAINTLY RABBI

So famous was Rabbi Kook's piety, saintliness and mystical love of God, that legends began to grow up about him.

One story is told by a rabbi who visited Rabbi Kook late one evening to discuss a serious problem. When the visitor knocked, he got no answer. Seeing that the door was unlocked, he pushed it open just enough to see the saintly rabbi poring over the pages of the mystical book, the *Zohar.* He reported that he had seen a streak of light emanating from the body of the ageing saint as he studied.

Another tale is told about a friend who invited the rabbi to walk with him to the synagogue for evening prayers.

"I will follow you in just a moment," answered Rabbi Kook. "I am so much afire with the love of God that if I should go with you to the synagogue right now, I might be totally consumed. First I must take a walk and cool off."

When Rabbi Kook preached sermons on the greatness of God and His Torah, he would become so enthralled and enraptured that it seemed as though the very spirit of God were speaking through him.

One evening during the holiday of *Shavuot* (the Feast of Weeks), which comes seven weeks after Passover and commemorates the giving of the Ten Commandments to Moses at Mount Sinai, Rabbi Kook began to preach his sermon at nine o'clock and did not finish until dawn.

On the festival of *Simhat Torah* (the Rejoicing of the Torah) he danced with the Scroll of the Torah in his arms for so many hours that he exhausted the young *Halutzim* (pioneers) and *Yeshiva* students who were with him. He often showed super-human strength, physically and spiritually.

On many occasions, in the heat of his great inspiration, Rabbi Kook would set down his thoughts on paper, both in poetic and prose form. Many of his religious poems are recited today by Jews all over the world. In a recent edition of the Holy Day prayerbook issued by the Conservative Movement in America, many of Rabbi Kook's writings have been included.

Because of the many accomplishments of the Chief Rabbi and the respect he won from all groups of Jews, he was given many unofficial titles. One of them was "High Priest of the Rebirth." Even though he did not live to fulfill his dream of serving God as a priest in the restored temple, he did become one of the most outstanding prophetic spirits of his people. In a way he was the Jewish people's "unofficial High Priest."

One title bestowed upon him was taken from the first letters of his Hebrew name —*R*abbi *A*braham *H*akohen. The initials of this name spell out the Hebrew word *Ro-eh,* meaning "visionary." Only one other person in Jewish tradition is known as "visionary." This was the great prophet Samuel in the Bible. Samuel was lauded in Scripture because he was like Moses and Aaron, both prophet and priest.

These are only some of the qualities which this modern visionary possessed. He was a priest, *Kohen,* by birth and aspiration; he was a prophet by virtue of his piety, and his dedication to God, Torah, the Jewish people and Eretz Yisrael.

As prophet, priest, scholar, educator, philosoper, and mystic, he was one of the great and noble lights in the Jewish world of the twentieth century.

When he reached his seventieth birthday, a consuming disease began to ravage his body. But even through his period of prolonged sickness, he proved himself to be a true saint.

22

END DRAWS NEAR

In January, 1935, Rabbi Kook began to feel that the many great battles he had fought – such as the Wailing Wall dispute and the Stavsky trial – were taking their toll on his health.

He felt himself growing ill. Accompanying his bad health was excruciating pain. He finally consented to his wife's pleading to have a doctor examine him. The physician feared that his illness was serious and wanted a specialist brought in to confirm the diagnosis.

Baron Rothschild was notified in Paris, and he sent his personal physician from France, Professor Ben-Sod. After a thorough examination, the doctor stepped outside the patient's bedroom and called aside Mrs. Kook.

"I am afraid that the news is bad," he said, trying to be as gentle as possible. "His mind is keen, his energy seems unabated and yet he is physically failing. His body is being consumed by disease. His fever is so high I don't know how he can possibly go on. He is like the burning bush mentioned in the Torah, aflame with fire yet not consumed."

Chief Rabbi Kook was dying from cancer. He had less than a year to live. He would never reach his seventy-first birthday.

His family and friends tried to keep the news from him and told him it was only a temporary intestinal infection, which would clear up soon.

But Rabbi Kook was a very keen student of human nature, and could read more from the faces of his friends and loved ones than they were willing to tell him.

Yet, despite his intense pain, he did not cease helping anyone who requested his advice or aid.

A young man came to his house and requested help in getting permission to take a trip abroad. In order to help him, Rabbi Kook had to go to several different government offices in Jerusalem, which would require more travel than his doctors had permitted him. Yet he insisted on helping the young man. He wrapped water bottles around his waist to dull the pain and scurried through the streets of the Holy City with the bottles flapping against his body. He reached the officials in time to help the young man.

By June, 1935, his strength had ebbed even more. But he longed to celebrate the festival of *Shavuot.* Instead of opening the doors of his home to the throng outside, as was his custom, he could permit only a few to enter.

The rabbi could see sadness in their eyes as they witnessed his sickly condition. He tried to cheer them up.

"Don't be sad, my good friends," he told them. "Judaism requires us to fulfill the commandment of visiting the sick as a *mitzvah,* a joyful deed. After all, suffering is a divine gift. Nobody can know how thankful he should be to God for the sufferings that come to him, since only through such pain can one reach the highest levels of the love of God."

When the Hebrew month of *Tammuz* arrived that summer, Rabbi Kook offered a special prayer as his colleagues gathered around him.

"May it be Thy will," he prayed from his sick bed, "that

this month be reversed from sadness to joy, from sickness to health, and may its constellation be reversed."

For a few moments his friends were perplexed. "What kind of a prayer is that?" they muttered under their breath. "Why is he praying that the constellation be reversed?"

Suddenly one of the rabbis spoke out. "The constellation of *Tammuz* is Cancer. Rabbi Kook is trying to tell us in his own subtle way that he knows what his sickness is. God have mercy on him."

The Chief Rabbi's only son, Rabbi Tzvi Yehuda Kook, tried to screen the mail each day to prevent his ailing father from seeing letters which would arouse his emotions and worsen his condition. But whenever the elder rabbi saw his son's face, he could tell if something was being withheld from him.

"Let me have the rest of the mail," he would plead. "I cannot lie here and let my fellow man suffer when I can be of assistance."

One letter was from a famous rabbi in Vienna, describing a horrible move by the Austrian government to clear away a Jewish cemetery for the construction of a sports stadium. All the Jewish graves there would be desecrated. The Vienna rabbi asked Rabbi Kook to write to the British consul of Palestine to act in protest against this vile sacrilege.

Rabbi Kook sat up in his bed and with great strain dictated the letter. The next day he called a meeting of all the rabbis in Jerusalem, in his home, to plan further in preventing this act of desecration.

On another occasion, Rabbi Kook was resting in bed late at night when a knock was heard at the door. He listened attentively to the caller's voice as his wife opened the door.

"I must see the Rabbi immediately," said a frightened voice.

"But he is ill, and it is late," answered Mrs. Kook, protectively. "Can't it wait until tomorrow?"

"Let him come in, Rivka," shouted the sick man from his bedroom. "If it were not an emergency he would not come at this late hour."

The young bearded man entered and sat down on a chair next to the bed. "I do not recognize you," said Rabbi Kook. "Are you a Jerusalemite?"

"Yes, I am, Rabbi," answered the man.

"Are you a Yeshiva student?"

"Yes, I am, Rabbi."

"Then how is it that I do not know your face?"

The young man turned his head to the floor in shame. He could scarcely bring a sound from his throat. "I. . . I. . . I am a student at the *Agudah Yeshiva* that has been protesting your appointment as Chief Rabbi all these years. I came late at night so no one would recognize me entering your house."

"How can I help you, my son?" said Rabbi Kook in a soothing voice, trying to help the young man overcome his embarrassment.

"You see, Rabbi, my daughter has broken her back in an accident. The doctors tell me she must be taken to Europe for an operation. We are poor and cannot afford these great expenses. I am told that a letter of recommendation from you will open wide many doors for me on the Continent."

"Bring me pen and paper, please, Rivka," he said to his patient wife. He began to scratch these words on the paper: "This will introduce a young man who is of the finest character, a resident of our Holy City, Jerusalem, a learned student of the Law, and a man worthy of the Torah. Any courtesy extended to him will be looked upon by me as a favor to the Chief Rabbi himself . . ."

The young man looked at the words, written in a shaky handwriting. His face gleamed with joy and tears filled his eyes as he now realized the kind of man he had maligned so often.

"We are both students of the Torah, my son," said Rabbi Kook. "You know that in the Book of Leviticus it says, 'You shall not take revenge and you shall not bear a grudge.' Go now, and God bless you and your family with good health."

23

A SAINTLY DEATH

The last Friday evening of Rabbi Kook's life was only a week before the Nineteenth World Zionist Congress in Switzerland. He urged everyone who visited him to attend the convention and participate in it fully.

To some people, the Zionists were "forcing God's hand." They felt that the Jewish people should wait for *God* to bring them back to their homeland.

Rabbi Kook denounced this view. "How can one not become a Zionist, seeing that God himself has chosen Zion? We are God's partners in creation, and must help Him do His work." He sent a message to the Congress wishing them well, asking that they help preserve the Jewish way of life, particularly the observance of the Sabbath day.

As the summer was drawing to an end, the Hebrew month of *Elul* was ushered in. *Elul* is the month before the Jewish New Year, *Rosh Hashana.* Throughout this month, Jews are required to hear the blast of the *shofar* (Ram's Horn), to induce the mood of repentance.

By *Elul,* Rabbi Kook was placed in a hospital in the throes of death. Nevertheless, he insisted on blowing the *shofar.*

"I have fulfilled all of the laws of our Torah up till now. I do not intend to give up at this point when I am so close to the end of the road."

His son, Rabbi Tzvi Yehuda Kook, was upset by his father's stubborn insistence on blowing the *shofar.* He remembered in years past how emotional his father became during this moving ceremony. It would be too much for him now. He pleaded with his father to relent, but to no avail.

Next, his doctors tried to dissuade him. His weakened condition, they warned him, would not be able to sustain the strain of such a blast.

But Rabbi Kook would not change his mind. Finally, his son had an idea.

"Father," said Rabbi Tzvi Yehuda, "you know that there are other patients in this hospital. The blast of the *shofar* will disturb them and prevent them from getting well."

"I never thought of that," said Rabbi Kook. This was the only argument that convinced him.

When word spread that his hours were numbered, Yeshiva students all over Jerusalem and Palestine prayed from the Book of Psalms for divine healing.

A delegation of rabbinical students stood at the Wailing Wall, so dear to the heart of their master, and poured out their hearts to God for divine mercy on the soul of His most devoted servant.

On the third day of *Elul*, 1935, his condition grew extremely grave. The renowned physician, Dr. Herman Zondak of the Hebrew University medical staff, was called to his bedside.

Dr. Zondak was not an observant Jew. When the doctor leaned over the bed to take the rabbi's pulse, the patient whispered to him, "I still look forward to the day when the Jews who are *great* will become great *Jews.*"

With his last spurt of strength, Rabbi Kook repeated the

ancient watchword of Israel, recited throughout the generations by Jews on their deathbed, "Shema Yisrael, Adonai Elohenu, Adonai Ehad." "Hear O Israel, the Lord is our God, the Lord is one."

With the word "Ehad" his soul departed.

A silent gloom spread across the hospital room. Amidst sorrowful tears, Rabbi Tzvi Yehuda observed that the day of his father's death was the third day of the Hebrew month of *Elul*.

"My father first arrived as Chief Rabbi of Jerusalem on the third day of *Elul*, sixteen years ago. That is when his life really began. And on the third day of *Elul* his life ended. Blessed be the Righteous Judge."

On hearing the news, Jews all over the world mourned the passing of their great spiritual leader.

Although Jews in every country were deeply affected by the passing of this great saint, nowhere were people more grieved than in the Holy City itself, Jerusalem.

There, a memorial meeting was held. One of the city's leaders rose to speak words of praise in memory of their first Chief Rabbi.

"We have lost the High Priest of the generation of Jewish Rebirth."

About the Author

Dov Peretz Elkins is rabbi at The Jewish Center, Princeton, New Jersey. He is a graduate of Gratz College for Hebrew Teachers, received his B.A. from Temple University, and earned an M.H.L. from the Jewish Theological Seminary. He was ordained as a rabbi in 1964 and received his doctorate in counseling and humanistic education at Colgate Rochester Divinity School. He has contributed articles to such journals as *Judaism*, *Religious Education*, and *The Reconstructionist* and has written twenty books, including a collection of readings on the High Holidays, *Moments of Transcendence: Inspirational Readings for Rosh Hashanah* and *Moments of Transcendence: Inspirational Readings for Yom Kippur*. Rabbi Elkins and his wife, Maxine, reside in Princeton, New Jersey, with their children.